Spotlight on Young Children and FAMILIES

Each issue of *Young Children*, NAEYC's award-winning journal, includes a cluster of articles on a topic of special interest and importance to the early childhood community. Most of the selections in this book originally appeared in the January 2006 issue of *Young Children*, vol. 61, no. 1, in the cluster "Supporting and Involving Families in Meaningful Ways."

Gail Wentworth's "Family Involvement in an International School: Piloting a Parent-Teacher Reading Group" is adapted from her *Young Children,* January 2006, article, and Tess Bennett's "Mapping Family Resources and Support" is an adaptation of "Future Teachers Forge Family Connections," also from that issue. Louise A. Kaczmarek's article, "A Team Approach: Supporting Families of Children with Disabilities in Inclusive Programs," was published online in Beyond the Journal, January 2006.

James W. Clay's "Creating Safe, Just Places to Learn for Children of Lesbian and Gay Parents" is an adaptation of his article in the November 2004 issue of *Young Children*, vol. 59, no. 6. "Partnerships for Learning: Conferencing with Families," by Holly Seplocha, was published in the September 2004 issue of *Young Children*, vol. 59, no. 5.

"Sharing the Care of Infants and Toddlers," by Amy Laura Dombro and Claire Lerner, is adapted, by permission, from C. Lerner and A.L. Dombro, *Bringing Up Baby: Three Steps to Making Good Decisions in Your Child's First Years* (Washington, DC: ZERO TO THREE, 2005), 61–71.

National Association for the Education of Young Children
1313 L Street, NW, Suite 500
Washington, DC 20005-4101
202-232-8777 or 800-424-2460
www.naeyc.org

Through its publications program, the National Association for the Education of Young Children (NAEYC) provides a forum for discussion of major issues and ideas in the early childhood field, with the hope of provoking thought and promoting professional growth. The views expressed or implied are not necessarily those of the Association. NAEYC sincerely thanks the authors for their contributions.

ISBN-13: 978-1-928896-42-5
ISBN 10-928896-42-1

NAEYC #288

Library of Congress Control Number: 2006937319

Printed in the United States of America

Contents

Cover photos (clockwise from top): Front cover/© Skjold Photography, © Ellen B. Senisi, © Ellen B. Senisi, © Skjold Photography, © Ellen B. Senisi. Back cover/ © Marilyn Nolt, © Skjold Photography, © Gigi Kaeser, © Ellen B. Senisi. Illustrations throughout © Melanie Hope Greenberg.

Supporting and Involving

FAMILIES COME IN MANY FORMS, from a variety of cultures, ethnicities, and belief systems. In some families, parents are the primary caregivers; in others, grandparents or guardians. All families want to help their children succeed. Some seem to know what to do naturally, while others appreciate some guidance. Each family has unique insight into their own child.

Family involvement is critical to the success of young children in early learning environments and beyond. Only when teachers and administrators welcome, respect, and value family partnerships do parents feel supported. Families then become more comfortable and confident with their chosen early childhood setting and their children are more likely to do well.

Here are some reminders of the basics of meaningful family involvement.

Make families feel welcome. Building and sustaining home/school relationships involves welcoming families into programs and classrooms, listening to their wisdom and questions, offering meaningful suggestions, and valuing who they are as families.

Upon arrival, greet each family and child with a smile. Bend to welcome the child at eye level. Share some pleasantries and invite parents to share a few details of their morning or the night before, as well as any special instructions. Mention what is planned for the program day. Children and families alike tend to feel more comfortable when they know what to expect.

Families want to know that their child is recognized as an individual. In the classroom they like to

see their child's name on cubbies, name tags, sign-in sheets, and artwork. This tells them that their child is acknowledged as a member of the group.

Display photos of each family throughout the room—on cubbies and cribs, on the wall next to the diapering table, on a low panel at children's eye level. Laminate pocket-size photos that children can carry with them to help them feel connected to their families while they are apart.

Upon enrollment or at the beginning of the year, pass out handouts describing the curriculum, listing the schedule, and suggesting ways parents can be involved. Let families know that they are important members of the teaching team.

Support children and adults during daily transitions. Some families, especially parents of infants or toddlers, feel guilty about leaving their children in the care of other adults. It is important to support the transition as the child goes from a parent's care and oversight to the teacher or caregiver.

Building trust is part of our job. Seemingly small interactions help break the ice: a tidbit from the child's day, an inquiry about a job hunt, even a simple "Have a nice day" upon departure.

Families are eager to learn about what takes place during each day. They appreciate information about routines such as eating, sleeping, changing diapers, and toileting, and notes and photographs about the activities their children enjoy (playing with toys, painting and drawing, reading books that introduce new words, writing letters and their names). Notes or comments on physical and social feats, such as climbing, smiling, or having fun with a special friend, are also welcome.

Ruth Ann Halacka Ball, MS, is project director for Oklahoma P.R.I.D.E., funded by an Early Reading First grant, at the Center for Early Childhood Professional Development, College of Continuing Education, University of Oklahoma. A former teacher of young children, child care center director, and partner with families for quality care, Ruth Ann is a consultant for family advocates and families.

amilies in Meaningful Ways

Families also look to teachers as sources of child development information about topics such as separation, toilet training, and books and activities to share at bedtime. Have handouts available.

At the end of the day, teachers' good-byes should indicate they are looking forward to seeing the child and family the next day.

Offer a variety of family involvement options. Families appreciate being asked or invited to participate in their child's education and development as long as there are a number of options from which they can choose. Not every parent or grandparent can volunteer in the classroom. However, they might be able to do things at home, such as repair broken toys or books, make name badges for a field trip, or help to put together a class newsletter.

Educators can invite families to visit the classroom, when feasible, to share information about their work and their home life. For instance, parents might offer a special food or song from their culture, assist with a class project, read to children, or share how babies are carried in their culture. When teachers and administrators encourage family involvement, children notice and feel a sense of security.

Establish and communicate written policies and procedures. Every early childhood program and school should have written policies and procedures for family involvement, fees, holidays, birthdays, illnesses, individual conferences, and other such areas. These policies can be spelled out in a Family Handbook provided at enrollment and whenever it is updated. Having clear written information minimizes miscommunication between educators and families.

Many programs find it useful to establish a mechanism for seeking input from families about program operations. Family advisory committees take different forms but usually include a parent representative from each classroom who reports information to and from other families. Establishing family advisory committees sends an important message: We want to hear your views because we know they are important.

Guide families in supporting their children's learning. Encourage families to visit and observe the many ways early literacy, math, science, and language skills are introduced and reinforced through daily activities.

Suggest activities families can do at home using simple everyday materials. Encourage families to help children build their vocabulary by having meaningful conversations at mealtimes, while doing chores together, or when riding in the car or on a bus. Create a lending library of bags or backpacks with books, activities, and other items for home learning. Collect brochures, videotapes, CDs, and books on brain development, parenting, children's books and activities, nutrition, behavior and guidance, self-esteem, health and safety, and other topics. Offer resources in English and in families' home languages.

Family literacy gatherings allow families and their children to learn and practice early literacy skills in a fun atmosphere. Possible topics are the importance of oral language, alphabet knowledge, concepts of print, phonological awareness, and choosing good books. Arrange for an interpreter if needed.

The articles in this volume enhance our practice by outlining a variety of ways to build and reinforce partnerships between educators and families. Among the topics discussed are

- Applying family systems theory in early childhood settings
- Conferencing with families
- Sharing the care of infants and toddlers

- Creating family maps
- Welcoming the families of lesbian and gay parents
- Addressing culture and promoting inclusion
- Working with diverse families to enhance early literacy
- Helping families support children's learning at home
- Running an early childhood reading group for families

— *Ruth Ann Halacka Ball*

Understanding Families

Applying Family Systems Theory to Early Childhood Practice

Linda Garris Christian

WORKING WITH FAMILIES is one of the most important aspects of being an early childhood professional, yet it is an area in which many educators have received little preparation (Nieto 2004). We spend hours learning about child development, developmentally appropriate practices, health and safety, playgrounds, and play. At times it seems that we focus on children as if they appear from nowhere, land in our classrooms, and merely disappear at the end of the day. We may ignore the settings in which they spend their time away from us, believing they are not very important. In fact, the home environment greatly influences what goes on in school. Much has been written on parent involvement (Ginott 1965; Henderson & Berla 1981; Epstein et al. 1997), and the literature includes a growing number of references to family involvement (Birckmayer et al. 2005; Crosser 2005; Diss & Buckley 2005). However, a limited amount of research (Bredekamp & Copple 1997; Couchenour & Chrisman 2004) directly addresses understanding of family systems as a key component of early childhood education.

To serve children well, we must work with their families. To be effective in this work, we must first understand families who are diverse in ways such as culture, sexual orientation, economic status, work, religious beliefs, and composition. Single-parent families, families of divorce, blended families, extended families, homeless families, migrant families, and gay and lesbian families represent some of the diversity in the families with whom we work as early childhood professionals. Yet no matter how different families appear to outside observers, all have certain characteristics in common; families just show them in different ways. Examining those characteristics helps educators engage families in ways that foster optimal child development.

> **Family systems theory can explain why members of a family behave the way they do in a given situation.**

Family systems theory

Family systems theory comes from the work of individuals like Ackerman (1959), Jackson (1965), Minuchin (1974), and Bowen (1978). While this theory is typically used in family counseling and therapy, much can be learned from examining it in the context of early childhood settings. Family systems theory has been used in trying to understand problems of students in school settings (Sawatzky, Eckert, & Ryan 1993; Widerman & Widerman 1995; Kraus 1998; Van Velsor & Cox 2000). The need for understanding family systems

Linda Garris Christian, PhD, is a professor of education at Adams State College in Alamosa, Colorado, working primarily with preservice teachers. Linda is also involved in local Even Start, Head Start, and other nonprofit early childhood centers.

theory in early childhood settings has been underscored by professional organizations in their guidelines for preparing early childhood and elementary professionals (NAEYC, CEC/DEC, & NBPTS 1996; ACEI 1997a,b).

A primary concept in family systems theory is that the family includes interconnected members, and each member influences the others in predictable and recurring ways (Van Velsor & Cox 2000). From our families we learn skills that enable us to function in larger and more formal settings, such as school and the workplace. Family experiences also shape our expectations of how the larger world will interact with us (Kern & Peluso 1999; Nieto 2004).

Family systems theory focuses on family behavior rather than individual behavior. The theory considers communication and interaction patterns, separateness and connectedness, loyalty and independence, and adaptation to stress in the context of the whole as opposed to the individual in isolation. Family systems theory can explain why members of a family behave the way they do in a given situation (Fingerman & Bermann 2000). It is critical to use these explanations to better serve children and families rather than for the purpose of blaming or trying to "fix" families.

While there are many aspects of the theory that could be applied in early childhood settings, I will limit this discussion to a few basics that I have found useful in my work with families and children. There are six charac-

© Ellen B. Senisi

teristics of the family as a system that are especially relevant for early childhood professionals: boundaries, roles, rules, hierarchy, climate, and equilibrium. Each of these characteristics lies on a continuum. For example, while all families have rules, some have many and others have few; some adhere strictly to rules and others are inconsistent. While few families fall on the extreme end of a continuum, they do tend to be more to one side.

Boundaries

Eight-year-old Miguel knows about the call to his house today. His after-school program director, Mr. Chin, told him that unless his spelling improved, he would be ineligible to compete at the city spelling meet. When the flyer on after-school classes came out in August, Miguel said he wanted to try pottery or chess. His mother insisted on his participation in the spelling bee and the challenging preparation for it. As he studied, Miguel felt a sense of pride in carrying on a family tradition. His mother, uncle, and older cousin had all won competitions when they were his age. However, Miguel has been frustrated by the rigor of the activities and the lack of time for other interests. By the time he gets home, a family meeting has already been planned to determine how best to help him to prepare. Miguel is nervous but knows his family will have good suggestions.

When Miguel's best friend, Mark, asked his mom which after-school class to take, she responded, "Whatever you want." Last year he tried and enjoyed swimming but got discouraged when his parents did not attend his meets. He signed up for the spelling bee this year, but only so he could be with Miguel. He isn't doing much better than Miguel, but when Mr. Chin calls Mark's family, their response is quite different from that of Miguel's family. Mark's dad takes the call and mentions it at dinner: "Mr. Chin called. It seems you're not doing so well with the spelling thing. Is there anything we can do to help?" Mark says, "No, I'm just tired of school stuff by the end of the day. Next time I'm going to try a sport or maybe chess." Mark's mom replies, "Sounds like a good plan, but what about Miguel?" Mark shrugs, "I did the spelling with him to keep him company. Maybe next time he'll do something with me."

Boundaries relate to limits, togetherness, and separateness—what or who is "in" or "out of" the family (Walsh & Giblin 1988). Some families are open to new people, information, and ideas. Family members tend to be independent and able to make decisions on their own. They value separateness and autonomy over a sense of belonging. Each person's identity is encouraged and respected. These families are sometimes described as *disengaged.* In other families boundaries tend to be more closed and restrictive; the families emphasize togetherness, belonging, emotional connectedness, and at times, conformity. They may control rather than monitor their children's friends and activities. Discipline is one way a family can enforce the boundaries within the family (Kern & Peluso 1999). Behaviors are seen as a reflection on the family, not just the individual. These families are sometimes referred to as *enmeshed.* An individual's identity is very much tied to the family when he or she is part of an enmeshed family.

Early childhood professionals should remain open when thinking about these two types of families. One is not positive and the other negative; the types are just different from each other. Families may show signs and degrees of each type; this may vary at any given point, depending on factors such as the age of the children, the family's economic circumstances, and the family's stage of development (for example, first-time parents versus a family with several children). Other factors, including the families in which the parents grew up, the social and political climate of the times, the culture and values of the family, and physical or mental health issues in the family, also influence the degree of enmeshment or disengagement. Over time families may change from one style to another. For example, during times of stress and crisis, a family that had operated in a disengaged manner may move toward a more closed system.

Miguel's family is closer to the enmeshed end of the continuum, while Mark's family tends to be more disengaged. Mark may sometimes wish his parents would become more involved with his activities, while Miguel may secretly wish his family would occasionally keep their opinions to themselves! The family's involvement in his preparation for the competition indicates their enmeshment.

In a conversation with Mark's parents about next term's activities, you may learn that while Mark's mother thinks sports would help his lagging physical development, his father fears self-esteem issues could arise if Mark struggles because of this lag. However, both feel that it is Mark's decision and they will support it. The family's disengagement works to foster Mark's independence and develop his identity, while Miguel's identity is closely related to that of his family.

As an educator, you would foster both Miguel's and Mark's sense of identity while respecting their families: share what you know about each boy's real strengths with the boys and their families. Help each child and his family to see the characteristics that make him unique and wonderful. Work with Miguel to identify family rituals, traditions, and values in which he believes. Help him find

ways to appreciate and honor his family's support. As Mark's teacher you may plan activities that allow his family to see Mark's uniqueness or activities that lend themselves to family involvement. Help Mark to see the ways in which his family does support his development.

> **Boundaries relate to limits, togetherness, and separateness— what or who is "in" or "out of" the family.**

Ideas for working with families—Boundaries

1. Recognize different parenting styles and family boundaries. Educators often perceive the family who comes to meetings and responds with active and enthusiastic involvement and participation (helps with learning or discipline issues, provides materials for a special project, serves as a volunteer) as more caring and as a "good family." The family who responds politely to requests but leaves day-to-day decisions and work on school matters to the child and teacher (allows a child to experience the consequences due to her lack of preparation for a quiz or forgetting her share item for the day) is seen as less caring and uninvolved. Build on family strengths and avoid labeling and allowing personal bias to influence your interactions with families.

2. Avoid stereotypes. Just because a child is of a certain culture does not automatically mean that that child's family is of a given religion, does not have legal status, has a certain discipline style, or has a particular socioeconomic status (Kagan & Garcia 1991). It is critical for teachers to become familiar with the cultural background of individual children and families.

3. Recognize that for some families *everything* is a family affair. Be sure to have enough chairs, snacks, and materials to accommodate extended families at events and conferences. For some families, an invitation to family night includes aunts, uncles, cousins, friends who serve as family, and even neighbors (Trawick-Smith 2005).

4. Balance children's activities and curriculum to incorporate both individual and group identity. Whether their families are disengaged or enmeshed, children need opportunities to experience who they are individually and as a part of a group.

5. Respect families' need for control. When introducing new ideas, materials, or experiences to children, involve families as well. Also recognize that some family members did not have positive experiences with education as they were growing up. While they may display anger, hostility, or mistrust, and these may be directed at you, the source may be events from the past. It will take time and persistence to build a relationship with these families. Teachers need to demonstrate that families can depend on and trust them to help in the education of their children.

Roles

"Lela, go and join the others on the playground. I'll finish the rest of cleanup for you. You've been a big help today," says Kathy as she hugs the four-year-old. Lela hesitates at the door and asks, "Are you sure?" Kathy smiles reassuringly. "Yes, now go play!"

Once on the playground, Lela pushes Sadie, one of the younger children, on the swing. When Sadie tires of swinging and goes off to play in the sand, Lela helps the teacher carry toys from the storage shed to set up an activity. Later, Lela mediates a dispute between two classmates. A visiting teacher taking anecdotal notes that day writes, "Lela's play was limited to 'helping' for outdoor playtime and much of the rest of the day. How can we encourage her to expand her play activities to include other roles?"

© Ellen B. Senisi

In all families, individual members have roles (Walsh & Giblin 1988; Tarnowski-Goodell, Hanson, & May 1999; Fingerman & Bermann 2000). There is usually a peacemaker, a clown, a rescuer, and a victim, although there can be many other roles as well. Each role has certain behavioral expectations. For example, if someone is the responsible one within the family, this person has a tendency to fix problems and take care of others, and others depend on him. The victim in the family is the person who gets blamed for everything. This person often acts out in ways that are sure to bring responses of anger, threats, and punishment.

Family roles can be carried over to work, school, and social settings. A child who has spent four years practicing every day to be the peacemaker will bring those skills to the classroom. While each role can have positive behavior, there can also be negative consequences. For example, if the responsible person in the family always solves the problems, others do not have opportunities to develop problem-solving skills.

Lela has a clear idea of her role in her family: she is a helper. Helping is a wonderful attribute and not one that teachers want to disappear. Having Lela teach others how to help is a way to build on her strength. To facilitate her whole-child development, teachers could set up a situation that does not lend itself to her helping anyone and encourage her play in that area. They could also refuse some of her offers to help, but with careful wording. For example, "You were such a great help yesterday, you deserve a day off today! But you can choose someone to do this job today."

Lela's teachers will need patience, consistency, and creative ideas to help her learn new roles. They can look for her other strengths and channel her energies in that direction. For example, Lela has strong fine motor skills; she could be paired with a child who is creative to design and construct new signs for the play areas. It is also important to find ways to share positive information with Lela's family that allow them to foster opportunities for new roles at home.

Ideas for working with families—Roles

1. **Give children ample opportunity for role play, in both structured and unstructured situations.** Children need to experience new roles as well as work through their current roles. Recognize the importance of children's cultural backgrounds in the roles they adopt (Noel 2000; Garcia 2002).

2. **Observe children carefully.** Many "problems" that educators identify are very role bound. A child who seems to be a magnet for disruptive events may be the child who gets

Family roles can be carried over to work, school, and social settings.

blamed for everything at home. Set up situations for that child to see herself in different roles. For example, engage the child in working with you to negotiate a dispute between two other children or allow the child to lead an activity.

3. Help families recognize their children's many and varied strengths. A note home might read, "Sally taught Ki how to put on his shoes today! She was a very good teacher" or "I appreciate Ricky's sense of humor. He always makes us smile!"

Rules

Jason teaches a toddlers' class. Soon after single parents Sam and Imelda met at a party, they began sharing rides and helping each other out on weekends. The relationship blossomed into something more than two single parents sharing the trials and tribulations of their two-year-olds. The two families have recently joined together as one.

As the assistant director, Jason needs to find out which families need child care over an upcoming holiday. When he broaches the subject with Sam and Imelda, he detects a stony silence. Finally Sam says, "I thought it would be nice for our first holiday to go away together with the children. My uncle has offered the use of his house in the mountains." Imelda chimes in quickly, "But I've always spent the holidays with my family here in town. It's just expected that everybody will be there. If someone isn't there, they hear about it for years."

Jason remembers a huge fight with his own wife the first year they became parents. It was about when to open Christmas presents. He understands Sam and Imelda's dilemma, but he isn't sure how to support them as a new family.

Rules are sets of standards, laws, or traditions that tell us how to live in relation to each other. Our patterns and rules for interaction have long-term and far-reaching effects. For example, if we believe in the predictability of life, we tend to plan ahead. If we believe what happens is out of our control, we may deal with circumstances as they arise rather than trying to prevent or avoid problems (Fingerman & Bermann 2000).

Rules may be spoken or unspoken. If we have been informed about a rule, we can discuss, problem solve, and make choices. If we are unaware of a rule, we may behave in ways that are not consistent with that rule. We usually

© Skjold Photography

find out about an unspoken rule by breaking it and then experiencing the consequences. Rules are often embedded in a cultural context; therefore, they can contribute to the feeling of cultural discontinuity that some children experience at school. When home and school cultures conflict, misunderstandings and even hostility can occur for children, families, and teachers (Delpit 1995; Noel 2000). Sam and Imelda are experiencing problems with procedural kinds of rules. Jason needs to support this family in a positive way without crossing professional and personal boundaries. There may be resources to which he can direct them.

Jason must be very careful in how he responds; he is not a counselor. Is this a simple issue, or is it one in which the family may need outside help? Jason can share his experience—that he and his wife found it helpful to talk to their priest, and that the center resource director has a list of local counselors that other families have used in the past. On a practical level he can acknowledge the importance of bringing both familiar rituals to the new family as well as new experiences that will bond the members together. He can encourage Sam and Imelda to keep talking and listening to each other so that they can determine what is important to each of them.

Ideas for working with families—Rules

1. Distinguish between home rules and school rules. When children challenge you on a specific school rule, it may be because it differs from home rules. Proceed carefully; it is critical to respect the home environment. For example, you may allow children to serve themselves at mealtimes, although at home their plates are prepared by adults.

2. Watch for unspoken rules, especially those related to gender, power, and how we treat each other; discuss them with care. While you may want girls and boys to enjoy cooking experiences, recognize that in some traditional families this may create a conflict. Discuss the skills, rationale, and benefits for children and families. You may uncover alternate activities that meet the goals of all.

3. Ask for families' input and assistance when conflict arises over rules. Explain the reasons behind school rules and, equally important, listen to the family. They can share information that may help resolve a problem or address changes that may need to be made in school rules. They may also be willing to modify home rules or talk with their child about the differences between home and school.

Hierarchy

Nancy, a preschool teacher, notices that the Hudson family has been rather short with her and almost cold since the last family meeting. Up until now they had been supportive and friendly. Puzzled, she schedules an appointment with Kate, the center director. Kate thoughtfully listens to Nancy's dilemma, and together they re-create the events of the last meeting with families.

After much thought, they focus on one activity. Several teachers had presented three curriculum designs on which they wanted family input. A couple of parents had given ideas, but then the communication stopped. In an effort to get things going again, Nancy had said, "Mrs. Hudson, you and Mr. Hudson have been active volunteers and observers of our curriculum for several months now. What do you think?" While Mr. Hudson offered several ideas, Mrs. Hudson averted her eyes and did not respond. Thinking back, Kate and Nancy remember Mr. Hudson looked rather startled and almost angry. But what was the source of this animosity?

Hierarchy helps answer the question "Who's the boss?" This characteristic is related to decision making, control, and power in the family. In some families, the hierarchy is a parental one. The parents share family responsibilities. One may defer to the other based on a specific situation or individual strength, but there is a definite balance and trading back and forth of power and control. Early childhood professionals may also observe family hierarchies based on gender and age and influenced by culture, religion, or economic status. At times there may be a clear and strong message but other times it may be difficult to discern. You may observe at the center's family picnic that the males are seated, served, and encouraged to eat first. In other families, the elder grandmother may be the deci-

sion maker, and everyone may look to her for leadership and guidance. The role of extended family in understanding hierarchy may be very important in some families (Morton 2000).

Early childhood professionals need to understand hierarchy because of the diversity of families with whom we work. Each time the family composition changes, there is a shift in family members' positions in the hierarchy. For example, one family consists of a child, a younger sibling, a mother, and a grandmother at the beginning of the year. After a mid-year marriage, the family home has the child, the sibling, the mother, the grandmother, the new father figure, and two new older stepsiblings. The hierarchy has changed. In families with large extended kin networks, hierarchy can be confusing to outsiders.

The Hudson family may feel that Nancy and her colleagues did not respect the hierarchy in their family. There are two issues for Nancy and her colleagues: prevention and repair. In terms of prevention, they could add some items to the information sheets distributed at the beginning of the year and returned by each family that respectfully ask about how the family would like to be approached in certain situations. Sample items might read:

Decisions about children in our family are usually made by _____.

How and with whom would you like information about your child shared?

We want to respect your family in our work with you and your child at this center. Please share any information that you feel will help us in these efforts.

Most important, Nancy and her colleagues should make conscious efforts to observe families and their children in center activities and social gatherings and in home visits to notice cues the family gives as to the hierarchy. They can become "family watchers" in addition to being "child watchers." For example, does a mother always defer to the grandmother on questions that the teacher asks?

To repair the relationship with the Hudsons, Nancy and her colleagues will need to be sincere, diligent, and focused on respect and what is best for the child and family.

Each time the **family composition changes,** there is a shift in where family members are in the hierarchy.

If conferences with the family don't elicit a response that allows Nancy to address the change in their behavior, she may choose to directly state her concern that she has offended them in some way. She may ask for their help in understanding so that she will not repeat her mistake and stress how much she values and respects the family as part of her classroom. She may communicate to them how vital they are to the success of the program and especially to their children. She may also ask if they have a need that she has failed to address.

Ideas for working with families—Hierarchy

1. **Engage in careful and keen observation.** Family watching is essential. Who signs the permission forms? Who returns a phone call? What family role does the child assume in dramatic play? Does a youngster assume that a male teacher is the boss of the female teachers? While answers to these questions are not always indicative of hierarchy, they may offer clues.

2. **Note the signs that a family's hierarchy is in the process of changing.** Be aware that children can respond by testing hierarchy in the classroom. A child who often leads at school may appear lost or unsure of herself as a new stepbrother takes her place "in charge" of younger siblings. Help her to reclaim her confidence through activities that allow her to experience success.

3. **Watch out for hierarchies emerging in the classroom and on the playground.** While hierarchy can lead to a sense of order and security, it can also lead to a pecking order and in the worst cases, bullying. Avoid activities that reinforce the same hierarchy over time. Vary activities so that different children's strengths are showcased.

Climate

Climate is about the emotional and physical environments a child grows up in. Some families compensate for hurtful or inadequate parts of the environment, such as living in a dangerous neighborhood, as best as they can (Nieto 2004). Other families have the best that money can buy, but the emotional quality of the home environment is not optimal for the children. The culture, economic status, or educational level of the family does not cause the emotional quality of the environment to be positive or negative. Emotional quality is related to beliefs about children and families. To determine the climate of a family system, consider the answers to the following questions: What would it feel like to be a child in this family? Would I feel safe, secure, loved, encouraged, and supported? Or would I feel scared, fearful, angry, hated, and unhappy?

Ideas for working with families—Climate

1. **Provide opportunities for families to discuss their beliefs about children,** what they want for their children, and how they support their children's development. Staff can facilitate at the events. These discussions help teachers learn how they can best support families as the families support their children (Delpit 1995; Garcia 2001). An additional benefit is that families often value information and advice from their peers more than through a lecture on good parenting.

2. **Create a classroom climate of safety, positive feedback and guidelines, and healthy sensory experiences.** Even (or especially!) if home environments do not offer these, children need to feel school is a wonderful place to be.

Equilibrium

It is critical for early childhood professionals to understand the balance or sense of equilibrium within a family. Changes or inconsistency in a family can create confusion or resentment in its members, including children (Kern & Peluso 1999). Consistency in families can be difficult to maintain, but it is essential to children's development of a sense of security and trust. Rituals and customs often keep a family together during times of change and stress (Fingerman & Bermann 2000). All families, even ones with ongoing difficulties, have a sort of balance that tells members what to expect. When there is change, positive or negative, it impacts the balance of the family. That is one reason change is so difficult to maintain.

For example, in a family where sweets, fried foods, and white bread are meal staples, a family member with a heart condition is told to change to a healthier diet. While other family members may wish to be supportive, it can be difficult. They may resent that their eating habits must change too, because preparing two meals is usually not feasible.

Ideas for working with families—Equilibrium

1. **Consider inviting a trained family professional to facilitate a discussion** when a big change or issue impacts a number of families (for example, a bond issue will impact the public schools the children attend). Families need to have safe places to vent, discuss, and talk about their changing worlds.

2. **Provide as much consistency as possible** when you are aware of changes within a family (a new baby or sick grandparent). This is usually not a good time

> Climate is about the **emotional and physical environments** a child grows up in.

to change the routine, rearrange the classroom, or introduce new staff. Recognize that in some cases, the teacher, the environment, and the school routine are the most stable forces in the child's life.

3. Encourage families to plan ways to increase stability and security. For example, parents may have to meet the needs of their young children while also caring for an older relative in failing health. Nevertheless, they can set aside time for a bedtime routine that involves reading a story and talking about the day's events.

Conclusion

The suggestions in this article are not absolutes nor meant to be perfect. Each family is unique, as is each teacher. Some educators are comfortable with direct interactions. Others of us need to begin discussions with an activity that demonstrates our connections to and caring for families before tackling these kinds of conversations. While establishing relationships with families before problems arise is essential, it doesn't always happen. We need nonconfrontational ways to broach sensitive topics.

© Skjold Photography

The keys to win-win resolutions are awareness, willingness, sincerity, and respect. Making an effort to understand families will open up opportunities for you to better serve children and their families.

> **Consistency in families** can be difficult to maintain, but it is critical to children's development of a sense of security and trust.

References

ACEI (Association for Childhood Education International). 1997a. Preparation of early childhood teachers. *Childhood Education* 73 (3): 164–65.

ACEI (Association for Childhood Education International). 1997b. Preparation of elementary teachers. *Childhood Education* 73 (3): 166–67.

Ackerman, N. 1959. Theory of family dynamics. *Psychoanalysis and the Psychoanalytic Review* 46 (4): 33–50.

Birckmayer, J., J. Cohen, I. Jensen, & D. Variano. 2005. Supporting grandparents who raise grandchildren. *Young Children* 60 (3): 100–04.

Bowen, M. 1978. *Family therapy in clinical practice.* New York: Jason Aronson.

Bredekamp, S., & C. Copple, eds. 1997. *Developmentally appropriate practice in early childhood programs.* Rev. ed. Washington, DC: NAEYC.

Couchenour, D., & K. Chrisman. 2004. *Families, schools, and communities: Together for young children.* Canada: Delmar Learning.

Crosser, S. 2005. *What do we know about early childhood education? Research-based practice.* Clifton Park, NY: Thomson Delmar Learning.

Delpit, L. 1995. *Other people's children: Cultural conflict in the classroom.* New York: The New Press.

Diss, R., & P. Buckley. 2005. *Developing family and community involvement skills through case studies and field experiences.* Upper Saddle River, NJ: Pearson.

Epstein, J., L. Coates, K.C. Salinas, M.G. Saunders, & B.S. Simon. 1997. *School, family, and community partnerships: Your handbook for action.* Thousand Oaks, CA: Corwin.

Fingerman, K., & E. Bermann. 2000. Applications of family systems theory to the study of adulthood. *International Journal of Aging and Human Development* 51 (1): 5–29.

Garcia, E. 2001. *Hispanic education in the United States: Raíces y alas.* Lanham, MD: Rowman and Littlefield.

Garcia, E. 2002. *Student cultural diversity: Understanding and meeting the challenge.* Boston, MA: Houghton Mifflin.

Ginott, H. 1965. *Between parent and child: New solutions to old problems.* New York: Macmillian.

Henderson, A.T., & N. Berla. 1981. *The evidence grows: Parent involvement improves student achievement.* Columbia, MD: National Committee for Citizens in Education.

Jackson, D.D. 1965. Family rules: Marital quid pro quo. *Archives of General Psychiatry* 12: 589–94.

Kagan, S., & E. Garcia. 1991. Educating culturally and linguistically diverse preschoolers: Moving the agenda. Urbana, IL: ERIC Clearinghouse on Elementary and Early Childhood Education, University of Illinois.

Kern, R., & P. Peluso. 1999. Using individual psychology concepts to compare family systems processes and organizational behavior. *Family Journal* 7 (3): 236–45.

Kraus, I. 1998. A fresh look at school counseling: A family systems approach. *Professional School Counseling* 1 (4): 12–17.

Minuchin, S. 1974. *Families and family therapy.* Cambridge, MA: Harvard University Press.

Morton, D. 2000. Beyond parent education: The impact of extended family dynamics in deaf education. *American Annals of the Deaf* 145 (4): 359–66.

NAEYC, CEC/DEC (Council for Exceptional Children, Division of Early Childhood), & NBPTS (National Board for Professional Teaching Standards). 1996. *Guidelines for preparation of early childhood professionals.* Washington, DC: NAEYC.

Nieto, S. 2004. *Affirming diversity: The sociopolitical context of multicultural education.* Boston: Pearson.

Noel, J. 2000. *Developing multicultural educators.* New York: Longman.

Sawatzky, D.D., C. Eckert, & B.R. Ryan. 1993. The use of family systems approach by school counselors. *Canadian Journal of Counseling* 27: 113–12.

Tarnowski-Goodell, T., H. Hanson, & S. May. 1999. Nurse-family interactions in adult critical care: A Bowen family systems perspective. *Journal of Family Nursing* 5 (1): 72–92.

Trawick-Smith, J. 2005. *Early childhood development: A multicultural perspective.* Upper Saddle River, NJ: Pearson.

Van Velsor, P., & D. Cox. 2000. Use of the collaborative drawing technique in school counseling practicum: An illustration of family systems. *Counselor Education and Supervision* 40 (2): 141–53.

Walsh, W., & N. Giblin. 1988. *Family counseling in school settings.* Springfield, IL: Charles C. Thomas.

Widerman, J.L., & E. Widerman. 1995. Family systems-oriented school counseling. *The School Counselor* 43: 66–73.

Partnerships for Learning

Conferencing with Families

Holly Seplocha

CONFERENCING WITH FAMILIES is one of a teacher's most important responsibilities. Effective parent-teacher conferences help support young children's development and learning by fostering vital home-school linkages.

Head Start Program Performance Standards, many statewide early childhood education standards, curriculum models, and instruments for determining program quality, like the Early Childhood Environment Rating Scale–Revised (Harms, Clifford, & Cryer 2005), identify regular parent-teacher conferences as essential ingredients for quality early childhood education.

In NAEYC's position statement on developmentally appropriate practice, the fifth guideline for decisions about developmentally appropriate practice—Establishing Reciprocal Relationships with Families—stresses that program practices are developmentally appropriate when "teachers and parents share their knowledge of the child and understanding of children's development and learning as part of day-to-day communication and planned conferences. Teachers support families in ways that maximally promote family decision-making capabilities and competence" (Bredekamp & Copple 1997, 22). Effective parent-teacher conferences open the dialogue and offer a vehicle for establishing and strengthening partnerships with families.

While schools and programs vary in the frequency of conferences, all successful and productive parent-teacher conferences share some common features. This article presents a baker's dozen of conferencing tips gleaned from my own experiences as a teacher and as an adminis-

Holly Seplocha, EdD, is an associate professor of early childhood education at William Paterson University in Wayne, New Jersey. A former preschool teacher and recipient of the NAECTE/ Allyn & Bacon 2005 Outstanding Early Childhood Teacher Educator of the Year, she has been in the field now for nearly 30 years. Having conferenced with hundreds of parents, Holly integrates building family partnerships into her work with teachers.

Photos © Ellen B. Senisi.

trator supporting teachers in building strong partnerships with families through conferencing.

1. Offer a flexible conferencing schedule. With their varying work schedules and other family commitments, not all parents can attend a conference during the day or on one designated night. Many parents juggle multiple roles. It helps to offer alternative conferencing times—such as early morning hours, lunch breaks, late afternoons, and early evening hours on different days. Some teachers may even meet at the local library on a Saturday to accommodate a parent or guardian who cannot come at other times.

2. Allow enough time. Conferences typically run approximately 15–20 minutes. For back-to-back conferences, be sure to schedule extra time (about 10 minutes) between them. This will allow for a conference that runs long or a parent who arrives a few minutes late. It also gives you time to jot down follow-up notes or prepare for the next appointment. If you know you need more time to discuss a special situation, schedule a longer period for the conference.

3. Provide a welcoming atmosphere. Avoid physical barriers. Don't sit behind your desk, and whenever possible, sit next to rather than across from the parent. Amenities such as adult-size chairs, soft music, and light refreshments help everyone relax. Know the parents' names; check records ahead of time to make sure you have them right. Don't assume that Maria Doe's mother is Mrs. Doe.

Nonverbal cues sometimes speak louder than words. Smile, nod, make eye contact, lean forward slightly. Let parents know you're interested and listening.

4. Be prepared and organized. Think about which items from the child's portfolio you want to share. Don't overwhelm the family. Select a few work samples that provide evidence of the child's abilities in several areas.

5. Be culturally appropriate. Effective communication is based on respect for others' values, attitudes, expectations, and culture. Keep in mind that childrearing values and practices are culturally embedded; differences may occur in norms, behaviors, values, role relations (mother/father, grandparent, other family members' roles and responsibilities), and communication patterns. Conferences provide an opportunity to learn more about diverse cultures and family structures and parents' hopes and dreams for their child. Effective teachers develop an appreciation and understanding of issues of diversity and where parents are coming from. They accept differences and avoid stereotyping.

No parent wants to be a *bad* parent. Suspend judgment and come to a consensus on goals and values for the child. Remember, parents are the single most important influence and resource in a child's life. Respect families and work toward bridging cultural differences and valuing diversity.

> Recognize and accept that there are **multiple avenues** for families to be involved in their child's education.

6. Stay focused on the child. The purpose of parent-teacher conferences is to share information about the child and ideas for fostering continued growth. While parents may tell you about other family needs and concerns, it's important to remember that you are not a professional counselor or social worker. You are trained as a teacher of young children and should make referrals to appropriate staff for other issues that arise. If there are no qualified professionals on staff, offer a list of community resources. You are also not their friend or confidant. Keep the conference focused on the child.

> Amenities such as adult-size chairs, soft music, and light refreshments **help everyone relax.**

7. Start by describing the child's strengths, interests, or abilities. Sharing positive examples with parents typically puts them at ease. You want to establish a connection, and the child is the link. Be specific: share an anecdote of something humorous or interesting that happened last week or today, or show a photo of the child's work or a work sample on display in your room. One teacher I know calls these positive points "glows and grows."

8. Encourage parents to share ideas and information. Conferences are a time to build teamwork and collaboration. Listen to what parents have to say about their child. Solicit their ideas. Parents want to be good parents and want the best for their child. Recognize and accept that there are multiple avenues for families to be involved in their child's education. Use the conference as a way to learn more about the child and the family. Successful partnerships encourage sharing and learning.

9. Refrain from responding to seemingly hostile or threatening comments. It's natural for parents to have concerns and even to worry about their child. Their ideas about the kind of role teachers should fill are colored by their own past school experiences. Remember, parenting can be difficult, and many parents have less formal training for their role than you have for yours. If the conference does get out of control, end it tactfully. Schedule another time to meet.

"We": The Most Important Feature of a Parent-Teacher Conference

The foundation for constructive parent-teacher relationships is frequent and open communication and mutual respect. When you are positively involved in your child's education, your child will flourish. Teachers prepare for conferences by reflecting on each child's interests and progress. Here are some ways you can prepare to actively participate in parent-teacher conferences.

Be willing and ready to share information about your child and family. Families are the most important influence and resource in a child's life. You know your child better than anyone else and have valuable insights to share with the teacher. Advocate for your child. Share things about your child's life at home—personality traits, challenges, habits, friends, hobbies, and talents—that you feel are important for the teacher to know. What kinds of things do you enjoy doing with your child? How do siblings relate to their brother/sister and vice versa? What kind of discipline do you use? What are your dreams for your child? What are your concerns?

Stay focused on your child. You are no longer the shy student who avoided the teacher's gaze. Nor are you the active four-year-old who seemed to always need the teacher's help to stay on task. It is natural for your ideas about teachers and their role to be shaped by your own school experiences. Being aware of these views can help you stay focused on your child and his/her unique temperament, individual needs, and special interests.

Never miss a parent-teacher conference. Use the conference as an opportunity to exchange information with the teacher and discuss ways to work together to enhance your child's education. If your work schedule makes it difficult to meet during regular hours, make this clear to the teacher and try to set up a meeting time that is good for both of you. If you can't visit in person, schedule a telephone call to discuss your child's progress.

Arrive on time. Teachers usually have a tight schedule for conferences—typically 20 minutes per child and family. If you would like additional time to talk, ask for it ahead of time so you and the teacher can discuss your ideas, concerns, and suggestions. Be considerate of other parents whose conferences will take place after yours. Remember that the teacher needs a few minutes between conferences to record and reflect on the information shared and to prepare for the next family.

Remember, children can hear and remember what is said. Young children often get mixed messages when they hear adults talking about them, no matter how positive the conversation may be. Arrange for a caregiver for your child or bring a family member to occupy him or her during the conference. If this is not possible, bring a favorite toy or activity to engage the child in another part of the room. Unless a child is expressly invited to take part, the conference is a time for you and the teacher to discuss your child.

Listen with an open mind. Concentrate on what the teacher is saying instead of what you are going to say next. Ask questions when you don't understand. If you disagree with a strategy, say so and tell the teacher why. Voice your concerns, but be open to suggestions. Stay on the subject: your child's progress.

Be prepared. Think about or write down one or two questions to ask the teacher. It's a good idea to ask the most important question first, in case time runs out. Remember, while teachers have specialized education, they don't have answers for everything. Teaching just isn't that simple.

Keep the conversation focused on what can be done for your child. When there are problems, parents and teachers need to stay calm and work together for the best interest of the child.

Stay involved. Try to visit the center or school frequently, not just for conferences and Back to School Night. Ask the teacher to suggest activities you can do at home to reinforce your child's learning. Look for opportunities to take part in your child's education.

Note to teachers: Photocopy this page and send it home to each family a few days before conference time.

10. Avoid using jargon and loaded words such as *immature* **or** *problems.* Terms such as *cognitive development, gross motor skills,* and *phonemic awareness* can be confusing. Use language that can be understood by all, and avoid generalizations and labeling. Instead of saying "Keron has strong classification skills," say, for example, "Keron does well sorting objects by categories like size and shape."

11. Share suggestions for at-home activities. Parents appreciate specific tips for doable activities that can help their child. Recommend simple activities that use readily available household items. Emphasize that everyday tasks like doing laundry and grocery shopping are vehicles for learning. Consider family budgets and available time. Don't expect parents to buy special materials. (And remember, not everyone cooks with a measuring cup.) Don't overwhelm parents with lists of things their child needs to work on. Focus on one or two specific action steps to work on together.

12. End the conference on a positive note. Thank all parents for coming to the conference. Stress partnering and continued open communication, and let families know their support is needed and appreciated. Engage parents in planning the best ways to assist their child. Express confidence in the child's abilities to continue to learn and develop. Save at least one encouraging or positive comment about the child to end the conference.

13. Take a moment to reflect and document the discussion and plans. Jot down a few notes about the gist of the conference and any follow-up needed. Assess

> Emphasize that **everyday tasks** like doing laundry and grocery shopping are **vehicles for learning.**

your own performance. Were you well prepared? Was the atmosphere comfortable and supportive? Did you use time well? Did you begin on a positive note? Did you encourage parents to talk and offer suggestions? How could the conference have been better? What did you learn that will help you foster the child's continued development and learning?

In addition to these teacher tips, a handout for parents and families—"'We': The Most Important Feature of a Parent-Teacher Conference"—can help them get the most from a meeting with their child's teacher.

References

Bredekamp, S., & C. Copple, eds. 1997. *Developmentally appropriate practice in early childhood programs.* Rev. ed. Washington, DC: NAEYC. Position statement online: www.naeyc.org/resources/position_statements/daptoc.htm.

Harms, T., R.M. Clifford, & D. Cryer. 2005. *The Early Childhood Environment Rating Scale–Revised.* New York: Teachers College Press.

NAEYC. 2005. *Early Childhood Program Standards and Accreditation Criteria: The mark of quality.* Washington, DC: Author. Online: www.naeyc.org/academy/web_ready/NAEYCAccreditationCriteria.asp.

Sharing the Care of Infants and Toddlers

Amy Laura Dombro and Claire Lerner

MOST FAMILIES TODAY share the care of their babies and toddlers with someone else—often an early childhood professional, a teacher, or a family child care provider. The family and professional must learn to work and make decisions together to support the child's healthy development and to ensure the family's well-being.

Although it is the norm for many families, sharing the care isn't always easy. Different people have different caregiving styles based on their cultural beliefs and values and their childhood experiences. It can be difficult for families to let go and temporarily put their child's care in another's hands—even if the other person is a skilled early childhood teacher. And it can be difficult for teachers to acknowledge and include families in the daily activities of an early childhood setting.

Sharing the care evokes strong feelings

No matter how much parents and early childhood professionals respect each other, sharing the care of a young child can stir up strong feelings. The relief parents experience knowing that their child is in good hands as they go off to work, school, or other activities is easy to handle. So too is the pleasure in knowing their child is going to have the chance to finger-paint or go to the park to dig for worms—especially if these activities top their personal list of things to avoid. But many parents also experience uncomfortable, hard-to-deal-with feelings like jealousy, competition, and guilt.

> Sheri is worried that her child loves her family child care provider more than her. She finds herself avoiding interaction with the provider and doesn't talk about her at all with her daughter.

Many teachers report similar feelings and experiences. This is no surprise as both parents and teachers develop deep attachments to the children they care for. It is important to acknowledge and explore these feelings when they arise because they can get in the way and prevent everyone from working together in a child's best interest.

Infants and toddlers rely on the important adults in

© Skjold Photography

Amy Laura Dombro, MS, is a consultant and writer whose work focuses largely on young children, families, and their communities. Amy is the former head of the Infant and Family Center at Bank Street College of Education in New York City. She works with a variety of national organizations, including ZERO TO THREE, where she coauthored *Learning and Growing Together* with Claire Lerner.

Claire Lerner, LCSW-C, is a licensed clinical social worker, child development specialist, and director of parenting resources at ZERO TO THREE. Claire writes a regular column on young children's behavior for *American Baby* magazine, and she is the coauthor of ZERO TO THREE's best-selling parent book, *Learning and Growing Together*.

This article, copyright © 2006 by ZERO TO THREE, is adapted, by permission, from C. Lerner and A.L. Dombro, *Bringing Up Baby: Three Steps to Making Good Decisions in Your Child's First Years* (Washington, DC: ZERO TO THREE Press, 2005), 61–71.

their lives to work together to keep them safe and healthy—physically, socially, and emotionally. The strategies and tools that follow can help teachers and families work together to support the development of infants and toddlers.

No one can take the place of the family

Most parents, at some time, fear their child will love a teacher more than he loves them. They arrive at the end of the day to find their child refusing to look at them or clinging to the teacher and communicating through actions and/or words, "I want to stay here!" This can be heartbreaking.

Families need you, the teacher, to help them see that the child's refusal doesn't mean he or she loves you more than them. By helping families look at the situation through the child's eyes, you can help them figure out what she is really saying: "I'm having such a good time here. I need a little time to adjust to the idea that it's time to go and some help to say good-bye." Or "I missed you so much when you left. Then Ms. Lucy helped me have a good day. Suddenly here you are. I need a little time to let go of Ms. Lucy and get used to being with you again." Through these hard-to-take declarations of love, children let their families know that they can trust them with their strongest feelings.

> **It's normal for parents and teachers to disagree occasionally over what is best for a child.**

Resolving differences

It's normal for parents and teachers to disagree occasionally over what is best for a child. Even parents can have different views about their child's needs or what parenting strategies are effective.

To let it go or not let it go (that is the question!)

Sometimes the differences about which a parent and teacher disagree are small and can be overlooked, especially if both are confident that the other adult is loving and responsible. For example, a parent might brush off the fact that his child's clothes were spattered with paint at child care because the teachers couldn't find his smock.

But sometimes "letting it go" is not so easy. When young children are concerned, even seemingly small issues can stir up strong emotions. One mother felt furious—and shared her anger with teachers—when the center's air-conditioning was broken for three days in the middle of a heat wave. She eventually realized that her child would be fine, but her anger persisted. "I don't think I am a maniac mom," she said. "Just one who loves her child a ton."

Naturally, handling disagreements is often easier said than done. When strong emotions are involved, the last thing anyone may be able to do is sit and listen with an open mind to the individual causing the upset. In these very charged situations, it may help to talk

Saying Hello and Good-bye

Here are a few suggestions to help make hellos and good-byes easier for children, families, and teachers.

• **Help infants and toddlers prepare for separations.** When a family plans to enroll their child in child care, they should visit the setting with the child several times before the first day. This will allow the child to begin to get to know the teachers in the safety of a parent's presence. If possible, the child can stay with the teacher for just an hour or two, gradually increasing time away from his parent.

Parents can play peek-a-boo and other disappearing/reappearing games at home and teachers can engage in this kind of play at child care. Adults can read children's books about separations and reunions with two- and three-year-olds.

• **Create rituals.** Upon arrival and before they leave, families can start to tell their young child a story or begin drawing a picture together. When they return at pickup time, they can finish the story or picture with their child. A special saying like "See you later, alligator!" can also smooth departures. A parent might give his child a special kiss that's only for good-byes—like one on her nose or forehead.

• **Step in to help families handle the separation.** A teacher can help a child begin an activity before the parent leaves. She can ask the child to be a special helper—to set up breakfast or take out the morning toys. The teacher can hold and comfort the child, and perhaps take her to the window to wave good-bye.

• **Help parents understand the importance of saying good-bye.** Saying good-bye lets a child know he can count on his parent to let him know what's going on. This tells him that his parent respects and appreciates his feelings. It also means he doesn't have to wonder or worry when his parent is going to disappear next.

over the concerns with a third party—for a teacher, this could be a supervisor; for a parent, perhaps a friend or another family member. Sharing the problem with another person can provide a chance to calm down, clarify thoughts and feelings, and gain some perspective. Always remember that the main goal is keeping the child's best interest in the forefront.

Because emotions can run so high, it helps to have a plan in place for handling differences between families and teachers. As one new teacher said, "Knowing there will be differences and having a plan for dealing with them gives me hope that sharing the care can go smoothly—most of the time." "Three Steps to Resolving Differences" offers a framework for discussing and resolving problems.

© Skjold Photography

Remember . . .

Conclusion

The fact is that young children benefit from the love and interactions they have with *all* of their caregivers—parents, other family members, and teachers. Having multiple caregivers gives children an opportunity to learn new things about themselves and others that can broaden and enrich their lives. And it can give families a needed break. As one parent puts it, "I know I can't give my child everything she needs. The way I see it, other adults in her life, including her family child care provider, fill in the gaps."

• Be aware of the impact your words and actions can have on others.

• Help families recognize the central, forever roles they play in their child's life. Assure families no one can take their place.

• Acknowledge the sometimes difficult-to-admit-and-deal-with feelings that caring together can stir up.

• Communicate respectfully and effectively.

• Understand, appreciate, and address differences.

Three Steps to Resolving Differences

1. Be aware of what each person brings by sharing feelings and thoughts about the situation. Choose a time to meet that works for everyone involved. If possible, arrange for another adult—a teacher or family member—to care for the child so the conversation will not be interrupted. Allow enough time for each person to share his or her perspective. While one person is talking, the other(s) listens, reserves judgment, and shows respect for the speaker's views.

2. Tune in to the child. All caregivers—parents and teachers—share what they know about what is going on in the child's world, her stage of development, and her temperament. They use what they know to think about what the child might be experiencing and what her individual needs are.

3. Decide on a plan that best supports the child. Agree on a plan and then try it out for a while. Arrange a time to meet again to see how things are going. Repeat the process if necessary.

> Denise, grandmother of two-year-old Tyler, was unhappy that children were allowed to leave the table to play before everyone in the group had finished eating. She valued family mealtimes and believed that Tyler should learn to wait. His teacher, Lilly, explained the reasons for this practice but suggested that they have Tyler remain at the table. After trying this plan for a week, Denise and Lilly met again to talk about Tyler's reaction to the change. When she heard that things were not going well, Denise said, "Tyler is a flexible child. I think he can learn that there are different mealtime rules for home and school."

Comparing Notes: A Tool for Making Decisions

Communicating is key in making any partnership work. But feelings about sharing care can get in the way of communicating information that is needed to make the best possible decisions about a child's care. When either a parent or a teacher feels strongly that the other adult is making a poor decision, it is important to talk about the concern—especially when it involves the child's physical or emotional health and safety.

Below is a tool to help families and teachers make decisions together that support children's development and well-being. To use the tool, both the parent and the teacher think about or jot down their answers to the questions in Parts One and Two. Then they find a time to sit down together—ideally without interruption—to discuss each of their responses. They then use this information to answer the questions in Part Three together. It is a good idea to do this every few months or whenever the teacher or parent identifies the need for better communication.

Part One: Focus on your feelings and reactions

If I had to describe *(child's name)* in 10 words, they would include _____

_____ .

What I like most about *(child's name)* is _____ .

What I find most challenging about caring for *(child's name)* is _____ because

_____ .

The activity I most enjoy with *(child's name)* is _____ because

_____ .

Three wishes I have for *(child's name)* are _____

_____ .

Part Two: Tuning in to *(child's name)*

(Child's name) is happiest when _____ .

The kinds of play and activities *(child's name)* enjoys most are _____ . I think this is

because _____ .

What upsets *(child's name)* most is_____ . I think this is because

_____ .

To comfort *(child's name)* I _____ .

I think *(child's name)*'s greatest strengths are _____ .

I think *(child's name)* needs help with _____ .

Part Three: Using what you know to decide how best to support *(child's name)*

What are our goals for *(child's name)* now? Over the next three months?

What kinds of experiences can we give *(child's name)* to help him attain these goals?

What special interests or skills do we each have that we each share with and teach *(child's name)*?

How can we work together to best support *(child's name)* now? Over the next three months?

Adapted, with permission, from C. Lerner and A.L. Dombro, *Bringing Up Baby: Three Steps to Making Good Decisions in Your Child's First Years* (Washington, DC: ZERO TO THREE Press, 2005), 67.

Mapping Family Resources and Support

Tess Bennett

WORKING CLOSELY WITH FAMILIES is a responsibility early childhood teachers consider part of their job. Continuity of care between home and school is important in early childhood education because when teachers develop partnerships with families, children's learning is enhanced. Intimate contact with families calls for teachers to assume the roles of listener, advocate, counselor, coach, child development specialist, and supporter. Understanding families' informal and formal support networks is essential to ethical and effective work with families on behalf of their child.

Just as social support plays a positive role in recovery from heart attack, stroke, and other illnesses (Ornish 1998), so it does for families parenting during stressful times. Bronfenbrenner's (1979) ecological theory explains that families exist in the context of their relationships with other people and institutions. These relationships can be supportive in daily life and in times of need; without them families may feel isolated and alone as they try to cope, having few resources to call on.

> **When teachers develop partnerships with families, children's learning is enhanced.**

This article describes the family mapping process as a tool for identifying family resources and support. Also called an eco map (Hartman & Laird 1983), the family map is a visual representation of the family system. Mapping can help teachers and home visitors comprehend the connections between family members and between family and community. It can clarify family strengths and stresses and indicate weak links in the support network, so teachers and home visitors can assist families in developing the resources they need.

Tess Bennett has a PhD in early childhood special education and is a senior early childhood faculty member at Eastern Illinois University in Charleston. She has taught in higher education for 20 years, 10 of them teaching an undergraduate course on working with families. Her research interests include teacher education, inclusion, and families of children with special needs.

Photos © Ellen B. Senisi.

Building a trusting relationship

As professionals visit homes and interact with families, building a trusting relationship is a primary goal. Families and professionals form trusting relationships over time through communication, empathy, and shared understandings. Finding common ground for discussion is essential. Here are some open-ended questions that are good dialogue openers when used in a conversational style, not as an interview:

• Who are the members of your family?
• Who lives in your home?
• Who are the members of your extended family?
• What is your family's cultural background?
• What are your family's strengths?
• What do you like best about your child?
• Who is in your extended family network?
• Who can you turn to for help?
• What is a typical day like for your family?
• What activities do you like to do as a family?
• What are your goals for your child?
• How are sibling relationships in the family?

When rapport is established with the family, family mapping can begin.

The mapping process

A strategy often used in social work, family mapping is appropriate for all families, including those from culturally diverse backgrounds and families with low literacy skills. The family map is a project that can be completed over several visits. This informal experience can lead to discussions about the family's view of important people and connections in their life.

The educator can introduce mapping while involving all members of the family. She should try to be relaxed and conversational, stopping to discuss each resource to be added to the map and letting all family members contribute. Children like to get involved by drawing on the family map paper and discussing their school and other activities.

Family, extended family, friends, professionals, school contacts, physicians, mental health care, worship, health care, recreation, and work typically appear on the map. The strongest connections are indicated by a thick line, tenuous connections by dashes, and the most stressful connections by a line with slashes. Energy flow is indicated by arrows going in one or both directions, depending on the relationship. In preparing to use the process, teachers can practice by mapping their own family.

Example of a Family Map

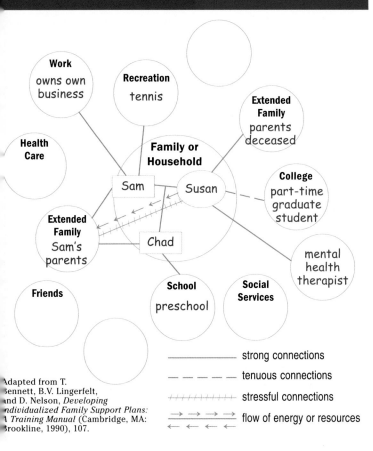

——————— strong connections

— — — — — tenuous connections

+++++++++ stressful connections

→ → → →
← ← ← ← flow of energy or resources

Adapted from T. Bennett, B.V. Lingerfelt, and D. Nelson, *Developing Individualized Family Support Plans: A Training Manual* (Cambridge, MA: Brookline, 1990), 107.

In the fictional family in the diagram above, the circle in the center shows the family members who live in the household—Sam, Susan, and Chad. Chad attends a preschool program, Sam runs his own business and plays tennis for recreation, and Susan is a part-time graduate student, which is shown as a tenuous connection. The family network includes strong connections between Sam's parents and Sam and Chad. There is a stressful connection between Susan and Sam's parents. Energy flows from Susan to them in the form of assistance with grocery shopping and daily living tasks. No energy flow is shown going back to Susan. Susan has a tenuous connection to college and sees a mental health therapist. Even though this is not a complete picture of the family, it gives some insights about stress Susan experiences. The Friends circle is empty, and even family and extended family support are minimal.

Interpreting the map

To interpret the information on a family map, it is helpful to know that the most consistent support comes from the informal social system, which includes family, friends, and faith community, among other organizations and individuals. The formal support system, which has less continuity, may include teachers, doctors, nurses, counselors, and others working for schools, hospitals, and community agencies. The people in these agencies may come and go.

For example, a child's teacher changes every year, so teachers are in close contact with a family for a limited time.

Because a family in crisis turns first to their informal resources, which are the most consistent and long-lasting, it is imperative to learn as much as possible about the informal resources shown on the map. A family with no informal resources, only formal resources, may lack important support and assistance in times of need. Intervention may be needed to connect this family to informal networks in the community.

Teachers' place on the map

Teachers become part of families' resource networks. This relationship can have a positive or negative effect on family functioning. For example, if the teacher takes over during a crisis, setting up appointments and finding resources for a family, the family may feel less capable in the future, when the teacher is no longer in the picture. On the other hand, becoming part of a family's support system may give the teacher insights about the extent of the family's needs, resulting in her helping the family take an active part in connecting with informal or formal support networks in the community.

Because teachers who are home visitors have a special relationship with the families they serve, it is important for them to clarify roles and expectations. Defining the relationship can be helpful, so all involved understand the limits. The teacher is not a friend in the sense of a friendship outside of work; the teacher is an early childhood professional who is intimately involved with the family on behalf of the child.

When families face special challenges, such as a child with cognitive delays or an adult with mental illness, addiction, or low literacy skills, they need special attention. Messages may need to be repeated many times.

Strategies for Working Effectively with Families

- Look for families' strengths and resources
- Identify families' coping strategies
- Build a partnership based on trust
- Listen more and talk less
- Suspend judgment
- Use colleagues and experts as sounding boards
- Build your own support network
- Reflect on your own behavior
- Admit and learn from your mistakes
- Change course when needed
- Write in a journal
- Learn about the family's dynamics
- Think flexibly
- Observe and reflect
- Show positive support for the family
- Interact honestly and authentically

Family-Professional Partnerships

Here are some basic understandings in good family-professional partnerships:

- The relationship professionals develop with a family has a powerful effect on the child's learning.

- All families deserve to be valued, respected, understood, and appreciated.

- Families do not usually get to choose their child's teacher.

- A relationship develops over time and with trust.

- Professionals cannot *make* a family do things their way; pressure impedes relationship building.

- Start where the family is, listening to family members' points of view, reflecting on what they say, clarifying their thoughts and feelings.

- Professionals often think they are right; however, a family may have a solution the teacher did not consider—that is the beauty of partnerships!

Teachers may need to use a team approach when working with community service providers. Understanding a family's limitations can help the teacher adapt communication to fit the family.

Sometimes a family needs a great deal of support—possibly more than the teacher can provide. The family may require other types of professional help. Teachers are not trained counselors or social workers; they need to know when to assist families in getting the professional services they need.

The family map can be revisited many times and updated and discussed as situations change.

Conclusion

The family map is a strategy to help teachers understand a family's resources and support networks. Some families and children come to early childhood programs with many needs, and the mapping process can help teachers understand the family dynamics and stresses more fully. The map can also help professionals recognize family strengths and resources.

The family map can be revisited many times and updated and discussed as situations change. It is an evolving tool that can aid teachers in developing a caring and trusting relationship with families, with supports, resources, and strengths in mind.

References

Bronfenbrenner, U. 1979. *The ecology of human development: Experiments by nature and design.* Cambridge: Harvard University Press.

Hartman, A., & J. Laird. 1983. *Family-centered social work practice.* New York: The Free Press.

Ornish, D. 1998. *Love and survival: The scientific basis for the healing power of intimacy.* New York: HarperCollins.

Checklist for Communicating with Families

When reflecting on your visit with a family, ask yourself, Did I . . .

☐ establish a partnership with the family and express the important benefits for the child of working together?

☐ use open-ended questions?

☐ paraphrase, summarize, and clarify?

☐ gather information by asking *what, where, how,* and *when*—but not *why*?

☐ avoid getting sidetracked?

☐ avoid jargon and technical language?

☐ notice body language and consider what the signals and cues mean?

☐ share positive comments?

☐ use encouraging facial expressions?

☐ anticipate family concerns and discuss them?

☐ acknowledge problems?

☐ express confidence in the ability of the family to solve problems?

☐ match my communication style to the family's?

☐ share information in a clear, concise way?

☐ break a problem into manageable units?

☐ support the parent in making decisions in the best interest of the family?

☐ give information that may be helpful?

☐ provide reassurance?

☐ coach the family?

Creating Safe, Just Places to Learn for Children of Lesbian and Gay Parents

James W. Clay

OUR RELIGIOUSLY AFFILIATED PRESCHOOL PROGRAM is located in an urban neighborhood. Celebrating diversity—including family structure—is one of our program's core values. These values include acknowledging the close ties between the child and family, recognizing that children are best understood and supported in the context of family, and respecting the dignity, worth, and uniqueness of each individual. Teachers at our school have provided training at other programs in our area on supporting lesbian and gay parents and their children.

From my own perspective as a preschool director, I decided to explore this topic. I approached parents and teachers at our school to see if my beliefs were valid on how to create safe places for children of lesbian and gay parents.

Parents' feedback

I sent out a questionnaire and conducted phone interviews with seven lesbian/gay-headed families at our school, which serves a diverse group of approximately 60 families. I asked parents questions about their expectations for their children and the issues and challenges they faced as lesbian/gay-headed families. As a staff we have developed a high level of trust with families, so I felt confident that their responses would be candid and honest.

The parents eagerly and openly answered the questions and even felt comfortable making suggestions for improvement. In some ways the results reflect what I presumed, and in other ways the results differ from my assumptions.

I assumed that the lesbian/gay families felt generally supported, but I was unaware of some other ways in which they desired greater connection to the school community.

As a lesbian/gay parent, what do you want for your child?

For each parent the initial and immediate response was always, "I want the same as other parents—that my child be nurtured and stimulated to learn." Other responses I heard can be clustered in four areas.

Emotional safety was the first of these additional areas of concern. Marlin, the father of four-year-old Marcus, stated succinctly and directly, "We want our son to have no experience of homophobia—active discrimination or exclusion."

The second and most often mentioned attribute that lesbian/gay parents wanted their school to have was *visible diversity in the school environment.* In diversity they

James W. Clay, MS, is director of School for Friends, a Quaker preschool in Washington, D.C. He has worked to support lesbian- and gay-headed families through staff development at national and local levels.

Photos © Gigi Kaeser from the traveling photo-text exhibit and book *Love Makes a Family: Portraits of Lesbian, Gay, Bisexual, and Transgender People and their Families.* Exhibit information available at www.familydiv.org or call 413-256-0502.

included family structure, race and ethnicity, adopted children, and transracial families. Everyone wanted to be sure that their child was not unique in the classroom in these categories. Again, Marlin stated it best: "While we are willing to blaze trails as adults, we want to avoid that for our son."

Deena, the mother of four-year-old Lila, said she wanted a school "where being gay is not considered weird." In addition, Josiah, the father of three-year-olds Mario and Nolan, stated that he wanted "the similarities and differences of our family to be noted and appreciated." In other words, these parents, like all parents, wanted their situations to be considered normal. Janis, the mother of three-year-old Jonah, said, "I want an environment that affirms my child's family and teachers who reflect this."

Lesbian and gay parents want their children to have *teachers with experience working with gay- and lesbian-headed households.* Ben and Bradford, the fathers of three-year-old Guillermo, said, "Having staff who feel comfortable with the idea of lesbians and gays as parents is of great importance." The two fathers gave examples of things they thought the school was already doing right, such as a curriculum and a classroom that visibly support lesbian/gay-headed families through activities and the use of pictures and photos. A couple of the classrooms have Family of the Week activities in which one child's entire household of individuals with whom the child lives comes in to do activities with the children in the room.

Regarding issues of family structure, race and ethnicity, and adoption, everyone wanted to be sure that their child was not unique in the classroom.

Although I did not expect it, these parents felt that *being a part of the general community* was important to them. Josiah said, "Because of the unique makeup of our family, I want Nolan and Mario to feel like they are a part of the group—not outsiders—and that their family is accepted and welcomed." Ben and Bradford said they wanted "to feel like we are a part of the school community."

I asked parents a second question from which several themes emerged.

What are the issues or challenges you see yourself or your child facing?

Deena said that since *much of the preschool curriculum focused on identity* (Who is in your family? What are your feelings? Who are you? and so on), she was afraid that Lila would feel like an oddity. In fact, Deena reported that Lila's friend Marshall had said, "You're supposed to have a mom

and dad," and Lila had responded, "You're stupid." Whereas this was Lila's most common defensive response to anything her peers said to her that she did not like, it also demonstrates her comfort with her family makeup and her willingness to stand up for herself.

Francisco, the father of four-year-old Rolando, said that he faced questions from his son like "How come Lee has a dad and a mom?" or "Where is my mom?" Francisco did not indicate how he responded to his son or how he wanted the teacher to respond, but Deena felt that the teachers helped children make sense of these things.

Many of the lesbian and gay parents acknowledged that *adoption issues are more important to them and their children than issues about having a parent who is lesbian or gay.* All the parents responding to the questionnaire had adopted their children at midlife. Along with adoption came all the added issues facing parents who decide to have children later in life.

Relating to other families was another theme reflected in the responses of the parents. Allan, the father of three-year-old Bill, said that his greatest challenge was building bridges with other parents, bonding with them, and expanding his community. Janis too said her biggest challenge was continuing parent/child connections outside the school and classroom. She pointed out that "acceptance is different from inclusion. People are nice but don't know how to bridge the gap."

Teachers' perspectives

To gain a greater understanding of teachers' perspectives, I interviewed Kay and Muriel, two teachers at the school who had been very involved in developing curriculum around family diversity. These teachers also had provided staff development at preschools in the metropolitan area on working with lesbian and gay parents. I asked them questions about building bridges and their successes and questions in working with lesbian/gay parents.

How do you build bridges with lesbian and gay parents?

Kay and Muriel were articulate and confident in describing the many ways they accomplished this goal. The first and most important method they used was communication—"We communicate to everyone that we are a diverse community."

At our school this diversity is evident in the environment—in pictures that celebrate diversity, photos of who we are, and books to widen our views. The teachers emphasized getting to know the children and the families and their goals, including details like what names the parents go by with their children. Their comments reflected their belief that lesbian- or gay-headed families are more like straight families than they are different from them. They felt it was important not to assume there is a typical family structure even among lesbian and gay parents.

The teachers recommended that families not be treated as though lesbian or gay was their only identity. And they cautioned that as teachers they need to be sensitive to the fact that parents may have fears based on their own life experiences.

What successes have you experienced with lesbian- and gay-headed households?

Kay and Muriel told the following stories.

Kay: Mia, straight mother of four-year-old Pearl, had been concerned that Pearl would learn about sexual activities or inappropriate words from the teachers and that labeling gay people might give her daughter stereotypical ideas about Mia's gay friends.

> **Adoption issues are more important** to them and their children than issues about having a parent who is lesbian or gay.

Kay said she assured Mia that the topics discussed and words used would be developmentally and age appropriate, as is everything in the school's preschool curriculum. Mia was happy with this response and, since she reported that other parents had been "talking," became an advocate for the teachers' curriculum with other straight parents.

Muriel: Annually, in my classroom of three-year-olds, I have a Family of the Week program as part of the curriculum. In introducing it at parent orientation in the fall, I specifically mentioned that celebration of diversity includes family structure. When it became the turn of one family with two moms, they made sure that they both came into the classroom together so that their family structure would be obvious to the children.

On another occasion I was engaged in pretend play with a four-year-old boy who had two mommies. While playing with plastic snakes, I told him that my snakes had two mommies. After a pause, the boy continued the play, pretending that his snakes had a dad. We both looked at each other knowingly.

The boy had realized that if his teacher could pretend her snakes had two mommies, he could pretend that his had a dad. The incident convinced Muriel she had successfully conveyed her comfort in working with all kinds of families.

What questions do you still have about working effectively with lesbian/gay parents?

Responding to my question, both Muriel and Kay wondered whether they do enough or too much to support lesbian- and gay-headed families. They still had questions: Would some lesbian or gay parents prefer not to be brought to the fore as "lesbian/gay parents" but rather to blend in as just another family? Are parents comfortable in saying to teachers "Please do this" or "Please don't do that"? What are parents' perceptions of what teachers do? Even in our school's milieu, a parent might not speak out if he or she felt uncomfortable with the topic, the two teachers concluded.

Kay also wondered, "How do I help staff relate better to lesbian- and gay-headed families they are uncomfortable with and avoid being judgmental myself if their thinking isn't as progressive or if they show prejudice?"

Despite support from administrators and colleagues, some staff may not be able to put aside biases and work productively with all parents. In these cases it may be appropriate for staff to seek other employment settings.

Summary

The survey gave our program a reality test for the assumptions of well-intentioned, well-informed educators and may be relevant for others in early childhood settings. Lesbian and gay parents' articulations of their hopes for their children mostly affirm what we would expect, but it is good to learn from parents themselves that our program is effectively supporting their families. It is important for educators to pay attention to parents' desires to feel like part of a larger community and have their child's school provide that sense of community.

These comments should help us all consider ways to more actively incorporate all families into the school community. At the same time, we acknowledge that as educators we may not be able to provide everything parents need or want. Even if parents attribute the absence of community to their being lesbian/gay, it is doubtful that being lesbian/gay is the only reason they do not feel a sense of community with other parents. Often, parents with demanding careers, some of whom happen to be single parents, simply find that their commitments leave little time to spend with other adults who might be supportive.

Our lesbian and gay parents said that the issue of adoptive parenthood was even more challenging than the issue of being lesbian or gay. Many probably identify more with other adopting parents than with other members of the lesbian and gay community. Some parents belong to adoption support groups—parents with babies from China, for example.

I find our teachers' thoughtful and well-informed approach admirable. As the survey's comments point out, teachers must continue to engage in dialogue with parents and with each other to get the right fit. Being dogmatic gets in the way. The experiences of our school indicate that continued dialogue is the key to working effectively with *all* families.

A Team Approach

Supporting Families of Children with Disabilities in Inclusive Programs

Louise A. Kaczmarek

Since the first day she helped her son board the bus, Lakisha has worried. She hoped Spring Valley Preschool could give three-year-old Jeremy, who cannot speak or walk on his own, an opportunity to learn and interact with other children his age. Jeremy had been in an infant/toddler program for children with disabilities in which a developmental specialist and other therapists came to the home. Lakisha had enjoyed the trust and sharing with the developmental specialist; she looked forward to developing a similar relationship with one of the teachers or specialists at the preschool. Her son seems happy enough at day's end—maybe a little tired—but Lakisha has many questions: is Jeremy making friends? why are his clothes often messy? what is his day like? how are the new therapists? should she be following up with therapy techniques at home? She has called Spring Valley several times and left messages. The teacher called back once while Lakisha was still at work, but there has been no contact with Jeremy's early intervention consulting teacher; the program hadn't given families that number. Parent-teacher conferences will not happen until October. Lakisha is making a list of questions to take with her.

Louise A. Kaczmarek, PhD, is an associate professor of special education and coordinator of the early intervention, early childhood education, and special education programs at the University of Pittsburgh. She was responsible for developing the model Family-Centered Preschool Project as part of the Pittsburgh Public Schools Early Intervention Program.

This manuscript was supported by Grant # H024B40033 awarded to the University of Pittsburgh by the Office of Special Education Programs, U.S. Department of Education.

LAKISHA'S ANXIETIES ABOUT SENDING HER SON TO PRESCHOOL and her many questions are not uncommon in families that have young children with disabilities. Children with special needs are increasingly enrolled in inclusive community-based settings—child care centers, Head Start, and preschool programs (U.S. Department of Education 1999). Like other parents of these children, Lakisha faces certain issues not even considered by families with a typical child.

Preschools, of course, offer families of children with disabilities the routine support given to all families, but their needs often go further. These families sometimes require more or different types of support, just as children with disabilities often require more or different types of classroom support than their typical classmates.

This article addresses the care and education of children with special needs in community-based settings. While early care and education programs often stress creating learning environments in which all children belong, they also share the responsibility for creating a community in which all families belong. Although federal law mandates parental involvement in the special education process, such as in the development of the Individualized Education Program (IEP), there are additional strategies for supporting families of children with disabilities in inclusive settings that can be extremely useful. These strategies go beyond the requirements of the law to include deliberate, coordinated planning among early childhood and early intervention staff members, regular frequent communication between home and school, and the identification of useful community resources. This article focuses on these support strategies because

> Preschools offer families of children with disabilities the routine support given to all families, but **their needs often go further.**

when added to the mandates required by law, they can make a big difference in the lives of families of children with disabilities.

Coordinated planning

Key to success in collaborating with families of young children with special needs is a commitment to coordinated planning and communication between teachers and early intervention staff. Only with teamwork can we reach out and support families.

Let's look at another scenario:

Two weeks before Marta's first day of preschool, Pine Hollow Center holds an orientation for new families. Rosa welcomes the invitation; she is a bit apprehensive about Marta's enrollment. Marta has cerebral palsy as a result of a stroke in utero. She is unable to walk independently and is delayed in other areas of development as well. On orientation night, Rosa meets Marta's preschool teacher, her assistant, the early intervention consulting teacher, and two therapists. She enjoys seeing the classroom and meeting other parents, including another mother whose child has a disability and several families who also speak Spanish.

The families receive a Family Handbook with information about the program's general schedule, its approach to curriculum, a calendar of upcoming field trips, and general arrival/departure procedures. The handbook includes an addendum from the early intervention program with the phone numbers and best times to call for all the personnel who will be supporting Marta's development and learning. Rosa leaves the meeting feeling welcomed and reassured. She is a little worried that Marta might not be able to maneuver her wheelchair into all of the activity centers available in the classroom and plans to call Kate, the early intervention consulting teacher, about that the next day. Overall, she feels welcomed by the staff and families and looks forward with excitement to Marta's first day in preschool.

© Ellen B. Senisi

Contrast Rosa's experience with Lakisha's. Although both mothers felt similar anxieties about preschool, many of Rosa's fears were allayed at orientation. Rosa met both early intervention and preschool staff, explored her

Key to success in collaborating with families of young children with special needs is a commitment to coordinated planning and communication between teachers and early intervention staff.

daughter's classroom, heard about the curriculum and typical day, and conversed with other parents. She left armed with a packet of information, including the phone numbers of all the preschool and early intervention professionals who would be providing services in Marta's program. (See "Planning an Orientation to Help Families Understand Their Child's Program," p. 30)

A successful meeting for families requires careful planning by preschool and early intervention staff who serve different functions and often operate under different programs/agencies. Their team efforts demonstrate sensitivity to the needs of families of children with disabilities and a willingness to provide coordinated joint support to the child and the family. Although not all collaborations will look exactly the same as this example, the underlying goal of any collaboration should be to make sure that families have the information they need to understand the totality of their child's experiences in preschool.

Planning an Orientation to Help Families Understand Their Child's Program

Advantages	Challenges	Suggestions
• Allows the parents of children with disabilities to meet early intervention and classroom staff as well as other parents of children with and without disabilities. • Enables families to explore the classroom layout, equipment, and materials. • Informs families about the curriculum, routines, activities, classroom procedures, and policies. • Gives teachers and specialists an opportunity to learn about family concerns and preferences.	• Could be difficult to schedule the orientation so that all families and all early intervention and classroom staff can attend. • Will require some extra preparation by staff before school actually starts. • May need to provide translation services.	• Prepare and pass out a Family Handbook; arrange for translations, if necessary. • Include biographical sketches of staff in the handbook. • Prepare a family survey to find out families' concerns, communication needs and preferences, and volunteering interests. • Provide the phone numbers of all members of the child's team and the best times to call. • Find volunteers to serve as translators in families' home languages.

Following Up with Phone Calls to Families That Miss the Orientation

Advantages	Challenges	Suggestions
• Lets families know they were missed. • Is a convenient form of communication.	• Some families may not have phones. • Could be problematic for families with limited English proficiency.	• Send home the printed materials distributed at the orientation before making the call. • Schedule a phone call at a time that is convenient for the family. • Use a translator, if appropriate. • Keep the call friendly and informal; encourage the parents to talk and ask questions.

Following Up with Home Visits to Families That Miss the Orientation

Advantages	Challenges	Suggestions
• Lets families know they were missed. • Allows staff to learn more about a family and child than other methods.	• Some families may feel ill at ease. • May be redundant if home visits are a routine part of the program.	• Offer options for meeting places other than the home. • Encourage parents to talk and ask questions; listen.

Establishing ongoing communication

After Marta's first day at preschool, Rosa can tell that her daughter has enjoyed the experience. Rosa is pleased, even though her daughter's new clothes are stained with paint and food. In Marta's bookbag is a communication notebook. In it, Eliza, the head teacher, explains that the book is for sending information back and forth between school and home and that the early intervention and preschool staff will frequently write in it to keep Rosa informed.

Eliza describes Marta's first day and notes that Marta played particularly well in the housekeeping area with another girl. Eliza apologizes for the state of Marta's clothes; they forgot Marta's smock when it came time to paint. She suggests that Rosa send in an apron for Marta to wear at snack time. She encourages Rosa to write in the notebook, but also points out that they can schedule phone calls or meetings, if Rosa prefers.

Rosa writes back thanking Eliza for the report on Marta's first day. She indicates she will probably dress her daughter in older clothes—not an apron—so that Marta will not stand out among the other children.

Marta's first day of preschool began in much the same way as Jeremy's. However, Marta and her mother were better prepared, thanks to the efforts of the teacher/specialist team. With the information Rosa received at orientation, she could talk to Marta about preschool, even show her photos of her teachers in the Family Handbook. The orientation and the resources from the meeting, along with the communication notebook, set the stage for regular and frequent open communication between school and home, a hallmark of successful partnerships between professionals and families (Dinnebeil, Hale, & Rule 1996; McWilliam, Tocci, & Harbin 1998).

The structure of classroom programs is not always conducive to easy communication. Teachers and other early intervention specialists must create an environment in which ongoing communication between home and school is valued. Many parents of children with disabilities need regular contact with their children's teachers and other service providers to monitor progress, address an ongoing problem, inform each other of issues that arise, or seek information or advice (Soodak & Erwin 2000).

Communication with parents of typical children often occurs when children are brought to school by their parents. These brief face-to-face exchanges serve to update families and staff about noteworthy events, activities, and concerns. Even for parents who drop off and pick up their children with disabilities, these informal exchanges are sufficient most of the time. However, parents whose children are transported to school by bus do not have these daily communication opportunities, and others may require more in-depth communication than can be conveyed at arrival and dismissal. Further, pertinent staff are not always present when a parent arrives to drop off or pick up a child. In such cases, alternative forms of communication are necessary.

> **Early intervention and preschool staff should talk with families to determine what strategies will work best for coordinating their services to a child and keeping the parents informed.**

Early intervention and preschool staff should talk with families to determine what strategies will work best for coordinating their services to a child and keeping the families informed. Potential communication strategies include notebook exchanges, telephone calls, conferences, e-mails, or home visits (see "Modes of Ongoing Communication," pp. 34–35). Inviting families to express their preferences lets them know that ongoing communication is a valued and expected part of their children's preschool experience. A coordinated effort between preschool and early intervention staff members is invaluable in developing a joint communication system.

Linking families to community resources

Rosa arrives early for her parent-teacher conference so she can browse the Family Resource Lending Library. She had heard about the library at the orientation, but because of her work schedule and Marta taking the bus to school, Rosa has not had a chance to take a look. Now she needs a sitter for Marta while she attends an upcoming church event. Because Marta can be a challenge at bedtime, Rosa wants someone with experience,

© BmPorter/Don Franklin

preferably with children with disabilities. In the resource literature, Rosa notices a notebook assembled by the early intervention and classroom staff. In one pocket are pamphlets from three respite care agencies. Rosa is perusing them when Eliza approaches to welcome her. After they join Kate, Marta's early intervention consulting teacher, for the conference, Eliza mentions that perhaps Kate could look into potential funding for respite care.

As they talk further, Rosa says she'd been thinking about what the future holds for Marta when she enters elementary school, during adolescence, and throughout adulthood. Rosa knows some people with severe disabilities hold jobs and live in group homes or even live independently. Kate tells her about an area support group for parents of children with disabilities that might be a source of information on the functional potential of children with disabilities as they grow older. Rosa asks for the phone number and e-mail address.

Through the use of the preschool's small resource library and in her interactions with Eliza and Kate, Rosa acquired information helpful to her and her family. Gathering information about community resources and parenting issues (such as TV watching or sleeping challenges) is often part of the support that early childhood centers provide to families. Classroom libraries, the public library, newsletters, and speakers can all inform families about resources (see "Strategies for Accessing Community Resources"). In addition to the usual topics of interest to all families of young children (such as recreational programs, special fairs and activities, child care resources, library information, government-supported programs), families of children with disabilities may be interested in family support groups, disability-related organizations, respite care services, advocacy and other policy-making groups, specialized clinics and disability-related medical programs, and groups supporting siblings of children with special needs.

Probably the easiest way for programs to provide information is to collect pamphlets and other materials from local, state, and national resources. In addition, the Internet is an incredible source of information for families and programs alike. The program can collect and disseminate a list of useful Web site addresses for the resource library. If there is a computer available in the

Online Resources for Families

Directories of Parent-to-Parent Organizations by State

Exceptional Parent Magazine—
www.eparent.com/resources/directories/p2p.html

Family Village Coffee Shop Regional Parent-to-Parent Programs—
www.familyvillage.wisc.edu/cof_p2p.htm

Directories of National Organizations Focusing on Disabilities

NICHCY National Dissemination Center for Children with Disabilities (state and national)—www.nichcy.org/search.htm

Exceptional Parent Magazine—
www.eparent.com/resources/associations/associationlinks.htm

Listservs, Chatrooms, and Discussion Boards

The ARC of the United States—
http://thearc.org/wwwboard/wwwboard.html

Council for Exceptional Children—http://ericec.org/maillist.html

Family Village Coffee Shop Traditional Matching Programs—www.familyvillage.wisc.edu/coffee.htm

Comprehensive Disability-related Web Sites

DRM Guide to Disability Resources on the Internet—
www.disabilityresources.org

The Family Village—www.familyvillage.wisc.edu

National Information Center for Children and Youth with Disabilities—www.nichcy.org

Center for Disease Control and Prevention—
www.cdc.gov/node.do/id/0900f3ec8000e01a

> Probably the easiest way for programs to provide information is to **collect pamphlets and other materials** from local, state, and national resources.

classroom, invite families to peruse bookmarked sites. (See "Online Resources for Families" for sites of particular interest to families of children with disabilities.) For families without computer access, print out selected Web pages to keep on file; update the information periodically.

Parent Resource Lending Library

Advantages	Challenges	Suggestions
• Contains items that reflect topics of interest to families. • Includes national, state, regional, and local resources of interest to all families, not just those who have children with disabilities. • Offers different kinds of materials: books, booklets, videotapes, audiotapes, training materials. • Allows family members to browse at their leisure. • Lets families know that you are there to support them as well as their children.	• Finding appropriate space. • Keeping the library up-to-date. • Setting up and maintaining a checkout system. • Finding/creating identical resources in Spanish or other home languages.	• Brainstorm and compile initial resources through team effort, then assign one or more staff members to keep the library updated. • Ask families what information they are especially interested in. • Make a basic list of contents that tells where items can be found in the collection. • Include local resource directories. • Collect pamphlets from agencies and programs in your area. • Look for and collect information from agencies that serve specific ethnic or language communities. • Collect and organize pamphlets in binders using pocket inserts, or house them in file boxes or drawers. • Post upcoming community events on bulletin boards or send home the information with the children. • Bookmark useful Web sites at the classroom computer station. • Print out information from Web sites or lists of URLs to add to the library.

The Public Library

Advantages	Challenges	Suggestions
• May have more resources and more up-to-date items than a center can acquire. • Offers public access to the Internet. • Has knowledgeable staff to assist family members in finding information.	• May not be easily accessible or convenient for some families. • May not have resources available in other languages.	• Work with your local library in setting up a resource section about young children, including children with disabilities. • Provide families with library hours of operation, resources available, and other information. • Regularly visit the library to see what's new and available.

Parent Meetings

Advantages	Challenges	Suggestions
• Can invite individuals from multiple agencies to take part in a resource fair. • Can invite speakers from local resources.	• Not always convenient for parents to attend.	• Publicize meetings well, including issuing personal invitations. • Participate in a community resource fair and advertise it to families. • Invite families and staff members from other programs or centers to hear your speaker(s).

Modes of Ongoing Communication

Classroom Visit

Advantages	Challenges	Suggestions
• Allows parents to see the classroom in action. • May provide opportunities for talking with staff. • Enables families to observe their child's interactions with staff and other children.	• May not be convenient if the child is transported to school by bus, if family transportation is limited, or if work schedules conflict. • Can be disruptive for some children.	• Make a videotape of the child to send home as an alternative to a visit. (See Audio Recording.) • Follow up the videotape with a phone call or arrange a joint viewing. • Ask for suggestions for making classroom visits and scheduling easier for parents and educators.

Newsletter

Advantages	Challenges	Suggestions
• Keeps families informed of ongoing events and changes. • Educates families about child-rearing, development practices, community events, and available classroom and community resources.	• May not reach families with limited literacy or English proficiency. • Can be time consuming to produce.	• Try a quarterly newsletter: the start of school, December, late February, and May/June. • Use simple publishing software. • Ask for a parent volunteer to help. • Include a Meet the Teacher column in each issue. • Include photos of the children engaged in activities.

Communication Notebook

Advantages	Challenges	Suggestions
• Informs families of their child's progress, activities, and demeanor; upcoming events; and other issues and concerns. • Keeps staff informed about home progress, including health updates, emerging skills, and family events. • Encourages back-and-forth interaction, asking and responding to questions. • Provides a forum for emotional support to families and staff. • Provides a permanent, ongoing record of the child—"snapshots" of his history.	• May not reach families with limited literacy or English proficiency. • Some families may prefer more direct contact. • May be inconvenient for some families. • Some families may be reluctant to write in the book, even though they may value the teacher's information.	• Use bound composition notebooks or journals so the book stays intact. • Date all entries. • Begin the book with an introduction and an explanation of its use. • Stress that grammar and spelling are not an issue. • Schedule a regular time to write in the books. • Include photos of the children engaged in activities. • Encourage use by all staff who serve the child. • Do not get discouraged if parents don't respond; most will appreciate your efforts.

Modes of Ongoing Communication (cont'd)

Phone Call

Advantages	Challenges	Suggestions
• Is a convenient form of communication. • Is more direct and interactive than handouts, other written communication, or recordings.	• Is problematic for families with limited English proficiency or families without phone service. • Offers less frequent communication than the communication book. • May be difficult to arrange with busy family schedules.	• Set up a regular calling schedule at mutually convenient times. • Provide families with staff numbers and best times to call. • Ask families for the best times and locations to call them. • Strive for two-way communication, not just a professional report.

E-mail

Advantages	Challenges	Suggestions
• Can be written at the convenience of staff. • Has a delivery method independent of the child.	• Internet may not be available to all families or staff. • Is subject to technical problems. • May require a teacher's time outside of the classroom day.	• Exchange e-mail addresses in the family survey. • Agree on an e-mail plan: how often, when, etc. • Find out how often families read their e-mail.

Audio Recording

Advantages	Challenges	Suggestions
• Use an audiocassette for sending and receiving messages with the family. • Is faster than writing messages. • Includes more information than written communications (such as through intonation). • May be useful for parents with limited literacy skills.	• Requires technology (tape player) in the family's home. • Listening to messages is more time consuming than reading messages. • Does not provide a permanent record of information.	• Find a quiet part of the classroom and schedule time to record and listen to messages. • Ask a bilingual parent to translate.

Parent-Teacher Conference

Advantages	Challenges	Suggestions
• Is a standard part of many programs. • Offers an opportunity to discuss the child's progress, the program activities, and the concerns of both family and staff. • Provides a written summary of the child's progress or status.	• Held infrequently—usually only once or twice a year. • May include only a limited number of early intervention and/or classroom staff.	• Encourage staff and families to schedule conferences as the need arises. • Celebrate accomplishments, don't just deal with concerns. • Hold at least one family conference with teachers and specialists together. • Engage translators for families with limited English proficiency.

© Terri Gonzalez

activities for children, emergency hotlines, and support for siblings. Many national organizations offer Web pages, e-mail updates, chat rooms, and Listservs on children and families with disabilities. Library and Internet resources can open up a whole new world for many families. (See again "Online Resources for Families.")

Summary

Only by working together can early childhood and early intervention agencies provide the kind of coordinated, coherent support that best serves families of children with disabilities. We must recognize that some families in inclusive early childhood programs require more or different support than do families of typical children. With a shared and coordinated approach, developmentally appropriate programs can meet their needs.

Connecting within the program

The parents of children with disabilities are a particularly valuable classroom source of information and emotional support (Santelli et al. 1997; Santelli, Poyadue, & Young 2001). They can direct new families to community resources, share their experiences, and offer advice on issues that they themselves have confronted. In addition to social events or orientations, programs can purposefully connect families. This usually takes a little preparation to avoid violating family confidentiality. Enlist the support of veteran families of children with disabilities to be potential mentors to incoming families of children with disabilities. When a new family arrives, offer to make such a connection. If the offer is accepted, then the program contacts the parent mentor, who then calls the new family.

Connecting outside the program

Many communities have parent-to-parent networks and support groups. In some, parents meet and talk with each other regularly, often about a selected issue. Other groups connect an individual family with a mentor whose child has a similar disability. Many groups sponsor newsletters,

References

Dinnebeil, L., L. Hale, & S. Rule. 1996. A qualitative analysis of parents' and service coordinators' descriptions of variables that influence collaborative relationships. *Topics in Early Childhood Special Education* 16 (3): 322–47.

McWilliam, R., L. Tocci, & G. Harbin. 1998. Family-centered services: Service providers' discourse and behavior. *Topics in Early Childhood Special Education* 18 (4): 206–21.

Santelli, B., F.S. Poyadue, & J.L. Young. 2001. *The parent-to-parent handbook: Connecting families of children with special needs.* Baltimore: Brookes.

Santelli, B., A. Turnbull, J. Marquis, & E. Lerner. 1997. Parent-to-parent programs: A resource for parents and professionals. *Journal of Early Intervention* 21: 73–83.

Soodak, L.C., & E. J. Erwin. 2000. Valued member or tolerated participant? Parents' experiences in inclusive early childhood settings. *Journal of the Association for Persons with Severe Handicaps* 25: 29–41.

U.S. Department of Education. 1999. *Twenty-first annual report to Congress on the implementation of the Individuals with Disabilities Education Act.* Washington, DC: Author.

Families, Schools, and Community Partnerships

Joyce L. Epstein

THE STRONGEST PARTNERSHIPS ARE TEAM BASED, with teachers, parents, and administrators working together to plan and implement goal-oriented programs, policies, and whole-school activities to create a sense of community between families and school. I have developed a framework of six types of involvement that can guide the development of programs at every age and grade level, including early education.

1. **Parenting.** Offer families assistance with parenting and childrearing skills, in understanding child development, and in setting home conditions that support children as students. Administrators should assist educators in understanding families.

2. **Communicating.** Keep families up-to-date on school programs and student progress through effective school-to-home and home-to-school communications.

3. **Volunteering.** To support children and school programs, improve outreach, training, and schedules to involve families as volunteers and improve family attendance at events at school and in other locations.

4. **Learning at home.** Offer suggestions and techniques to involve families in learning activities with their children at home.

5. **Decision making.** Include families as participants in school decisions, governance, and advocacy through PTA/PTO, school councils, committees, and other parent organizations.

6. **Collaborating with the community.** Coordinate resources and services for families, children, and the school with businesses, agencies, and other groups. Provide services to the community. For example, young children might entertain senior citizens or plant flowers to beautify a park.

Whether the focus is on reading or math or social interaction, children do better whenever teachers, families, and the community all work together to reach important goals for learning and development. Families and the community can be involved in ways that help children develop school readiness in math, literacy, social interactions, and other areas.

For more information on developing effective partnership programs, see **www.partnershipschools.org**.

Joyce L. Epstein, PhD, is director of the Center on School, Family, and Community Partnerships and the National Network of Partnership Schools (NNPS), and research professor of sociology at Johns Hopkins University. Her studies of family and community involvement connect research, policy, and practice.

Photos © Skjold Photography

Closing the Gap

Culture and the Promotion of Inclusion in Child Care

THREE TRENDS ARE OF CRITICAL IMPORTANCE as early childhood professionals prepare to meet the needs of children and families. These trends are demographic changes in the U.S. population resulting in the increased diversity of families' cultural backgrounds (Brewer & Suchan 2001); the movement toward inclusion and recognition of the rights of all children to be cared for in natural environments (Odon, Teferra, & Kaul 2004); and the increased prevalence of emotional and behavioral problems among preschool children (Koppelman 2004).

Using real-world examples drawn from the Models of Inclusion in Child Care project (Brennan et al. 2003), this article examines the interface between attention to families' cultural backgrounds and the ability of early childhood programs to be successful in providing inclusive care for children with disabilities and challenging behaviors. Nine child care centers across the United States participated in this research. These programs provide care for children with different types of disabilities and children with emotional and behavioral challenges alongside children without such challenges or delays. The ages of children enrolled in the programs ranged from birth to 13 years, although most children were younger than six years. Some families reported that their children had been excluded previously from one or more child care programs due to disruptive behavior.

Jennifer Rose Bradley, PhD, is a chartered psychologist (UK) residing in Dallas, Texas. Until recently she was a research associate at the Regional Research Institute, Portland State University, Oregon. Jennifer's work focuses on inclusion, transitions, and work-life integration. E-mail: bradley_jennifer@yahoo.com.

Peris W. Kibera, MSW, is a doctoral student at the University of Washington School of Social Work. Peris has worked in clinical- and community-level capacities with African immigrants in Oregon and southwest Washington.

Jennifer Bradley and Peris Kibera

The research findings from the Models of Inclusion in Child Care project indicate that attention to families' cultures is essential for the successful inclusion of children with challenging behaviors. Based on the analysis of more than 90 interviews with directors, staff, and parents, this article discusses how professionals' understanding of families' cultural backgrounds supports the centers' success in providing inclusive care for diverse children with disabilities or challenging behaviors. It concludes with five recommendations for early childhood professionals.

Inclusion and culture

The nine centers in the Models of Inclusion project (Brennan et al. 2003) were selected to vary in size, location, funding arrangements, and the population served. It was evident, however, that all of the centers shared a vision of inclusion that was crucial to their success in integrating children with disabilities or emotional and behavioral challenges. Inclusion was an intentional process that shaped the design and delivery of the child care programs. One staff member explained, "Families are a grand spectrum, and we . . . embrace them no matter what and do what we can to help their kids."

Center staff at all levels shared a philosophy of inclusion, and administrators and senior staff continually reinforced the philosophy through their efforts to embed strategies for inclusion in all center activities. This was achieved through an individualized approach to supporting each child and family. Staff worked to build relationships with families. They engaged in ongoing communication and problem solving to identify resources and agree on intervention strategies to provide the support necessary for inclusion even when children had challenging behaviors. Classroom activities were designed with built-in flexibility to accommodate children with different needs. For example, teachers gave advance notice of changes in activities to support children who found transitions stressful. Staff made efforts to build connections between the center and home for all families—for instance, providing children's reading materials in the family's primary language if parents did not speak English.

The work of each center was founded on a clear and explicit philosophy of serving all children and families. The values, principles, and practices that supported the centers' inclusion of children with challenging behaviors also supported the centers' efforts to work successfully with children and families from varied cultural backgrounds. For example, teachers used stick figures or other visual materials to give children clear information about desired goals and expectations for behavior. They used multiple methods of communication simultaneously to support children with difficulties in processing information due to cognitive deficits. This practice also helped children to overcome linguistic barriers and speech difficulties.

Early childhood educators and families may experience barriers in supporting children's learning and development when the children's behavior is disruptive. Cultural differences between staff and families can lead to additional barriers. Culture has been defined in different ways. One expert defines culture as consisting of "shared elements that provide the standards for perceiving, believing, communicating, and acting among those who share a language, a historic period, and a geographic location" (Triandis 1996, 409). Although there is no single agreed-upon definition of culture, culture influences our thoughts and behaviors and is shared by a group, passed on to members of the group, and changes over time (O'Hagan 1999; Greenfield et al. 2003).

One teacher interviewed in the research explained her experience of learning about cultural differences during her first year of working with children from Latino families:

> There were a lot of things I had to learn. Just the nature of the children, the things they would do differently, and the reasons behind it . . . The way things were at home was different from [my] culture.

She described the need to adapt her customary practice of expecting children to "look her in the eye" when she was addressing them, in recognition of culturally based variations in nonverbal communication and "looking down" as a sign of respect for the teacher.

© NAEYC

> **Culture influences our thoughts and behaviors** and is shared by a group, passed on to members of the group, and changes over time.

Cultural awareness

Although cultural differences are often discussed in terms of ethnic, racial, and linguistic diversity, staff in these nine centers also talked about the importance of other dimensions of culture, such as region or geographic location, religion, and socioeconomic status. One director described working with families from a rural area:

> [Families in our rural setting have] a very independent culture . . . [and] they're very reticent to ask for help. They're suspicious of outside interference in their family structure, and you have to gain their trust. If you're not from . . . that little geographical area, you're an outsider; they don't think you understand how they do things.

Cultural Dimensions of Families

Four dimensions of culture are listed here with questions that encourage further exploration of the influences of culture in your work. The questions can be modified for individual self-assessment, for use as a tool to explore differences among staff, or as the basis for discussing cultural issues with families.

Dimensions	Questions for reflection and/or discussion
Values and beliefs	How is *family* defined? What roles do adults and children play? How does the family make sense of a child's behavioral difficulties? How does culture inform the family's view of appropriate/inappropriate ways of dealing with problem behavior and guiding children? What is most important to the family?
Historical and social influences	What strengths and stressors does the family identify? What barriers do they experience?
Communication	What is the family's primary language? What support is required to enable communication? How are needs and wants expressed? How is unhappiness, dissatisfaction, or distress experienced and expressed?
Attitude toward seeking help	How does the family seek help and from whom? How do members view professionals, and how do professionals view them?

One of the challenges of understanding different cultures is that while some aspects, such as language or dress, are easily discerned, many aspects are less obvious. The research identified four characteristics of culture as important considerations when working with families from diverse backgrounds: values and beliefs, historical and social influences, communication, and attitude toward seeking help (see "Cultural Dimensions of Families").

Developing cultural awareness is an ongoing process. Several staff interviewed in the study talked about the importance of taking a positive approach and being open to continuous learning. One teacher noted, "If it's something that I'm not familiar with, then it's a learning opportunity." Staff described the need to learn about culturally based practices such as how family decisions are made and who is involved in the process. Staff intentionally sought to involve families in their children's care by providing varied opportunities, including open invitations to parents to spend time in the classroom, parent presentations to share culture-specific information with staff and

children, volunteer opportunities, parent information events, and regular social events with other families at the center. Building relationships with parents included efforts to learn about families by asking them specific questions about their cultures, such as what holidays they do or don't celebrate and their food preferences or prohibitions. In addition, staff asked families about their goals and expectations for their child.

When accompanied by linguistic barriers, cultural differences can pose particular challenges for families and staff. In her book describing the experiences of immigrant refugees in the United States, Mary Pipher proposes two simple rules for working with people for whom English is a new language: *Don't assume anything* and *Ask questions* (Pipher 2002, 353). The directors and teachers in the Models of Inclusion research echoed these rules, and noted the importance of resources such as translation services and interpreters to support their work with families. Families valued staff efforts to partner with them in exchanging information in an accessible way. One family member explained,

> When you are here, you have the possibility of sharing. For example, the teacher says, "What do you think? What are you going to do if you have a problem with your child in the school?" And the teachers explain to you in Spanish and English . . . what you can do. That is important.

Respecting cultural differences

It was evident from the Models of Inclusion in Child Care research that family involvement is crucial to the successful inclusion of children with disabilities or challenging behaviors, and that understanding a family's culture is essential in building relationships between families and center staff. However, cultural differences can pose challenges for staff and for families. Researchers identified two important potential sources of difference: norms of privacy and perceptions of child development.

Privacy issues

Programs used open-ended questions to elicit whatever information—if any—families wanted to share about themselves. One staff member explained that cultural sensitivity can help staff understand and accept families' different perspectives on information sharing:

> It is very difficult for [some families] to share information about their private lives. And we often feel that the only way we can truly do our job is to have all this information. But I think [we need] to remember that we have to respect what [families] are comfortable with, as far as what they feel like they can share.

For example, in some families, mothers did not feel comfortable sharing information about the family without a male family member present.

As noted by one director, it is essential for teachers to ask themselves, How can we offer support to families rather than make judgments about them? Understanding a family's culture helps staff to withhold judgment, to manage the frustration that can arise from differences, and to continue efforts to build relationships with the family and gain family members' trust.

Differing perceptions of child development

The second important issue for successful inclusion of children with disabilities or challenging behaviors is cultural differences in how child development is perceived by families and teachers. Cultural beliefs may have a significant impact on parents' expectations about their child's behavior and ability. One director describes some of the challenges that can arise when a child has a disability:

> [Families] are sometimes fatalistic in their outlook [regarding] . . . the potential their child might have. And [reluctant] to accept support in helping the child reach that potential. [A family's attitude may be,] "Well, this is the way he was born, and we just have to live with it."

The gaps that arise from cultural differences in professional and family perspectives on appropriate ways to support a child's development can lead to frustration and difficulty in developing the necessary partnerships.

> Cultural sensitivity can **help staff understand and accept** families' different perspectives on information sharing.

It is essential that staff take the time to understand how family members make sense of their child's experience and behaviors. Additionally, it is important that staff recognize the benefits families can gain from connecting to the strengths of their cultures and accessing the resources of their cultural communities (Hunt 2004). Parents can benefit from the support of other families with similar experiences

> It is important that staff recognize the benefits families can gain from **connecting to the strengths of their cultures** and accessing the resources of their cultural communities.

who share culturally appropriate information about strategies they have found useful—for example, strategies to help their children gain more control over their behavior by learning to manage stress and increase self-regulation.

Supporting the whole family

On the other hand, parents who have a child with challenging behaviors or a disability may have to deal with isolation, blame, shame, or other forms of stigma in the community. In our research, staff recognized the importance of providing support for the whole family as a way of supporting the child. One way teachers supported families was by creating opportunities for families to meet each other during parent education and center social events and by acting as brokers to connect families with local resources, such as health care, social services, housing, and agencies providing culture-specific services.

Research shows that families that have children with challenging behaviors frequently do not receive the support and services they need (Knitzer 2002), and when such families are members of minority groups, they are even less likely to have access to preventive and mental health services (U.S. Department of Health and Human Services 2001; President's New Freedom Commission on Mental Health 2003). It is increasingly important that early childhood professionals

© NAEYC

extend the skills and strategies they use when including children with disabilities or emotional and behavioral challenges to encompass the cultural context of the family. While children's needs change with their continued growth and development, an individualized approach informed by the family's culture is an essential part of promoting healthy development for all children. For some families that have children with disabilities or challenging behaviors, the support available through an early childhood setting may be their first opportunity to get the help they need.

References

Brennan, E.M., J.R. Bradley, S.M. Ama, & N. Cawood. 2003. *Setting the pace: Model inclusive child care centers serving families of children with emotional or behavioral challenges.* Portland, OR: Portland State University Research and Training Center on Family Support and Children's Mental Health. Online: www.rtc.pdx.edu/pgProjInclusion.php.

Brewer, C.A., & T.A. Suchan. 2001. *Mapping Census 2000: The geography of U.S. diversity.* Washington, DC: U.S. Census Bureau, Census Special Reports. Online: www.census.gov/population/cen2000/atlas/censr01-1.pdf.

Greenfield, P.M., H. Keller, A. Fuligni, & A. Maynard. 2003. Cultural pathways through universal development. *Annual Review of Psychology* 54: 1–23.

Hunt, R.A. 2004. Transforming children's mental health care in Indian Country. *Pathways* (April): 1–11.

Knitzer, J. 2002. Building services and systems to support the healthy emotional development of young children: An action guide for policymakers. Online: www.nccp.org/media/pew02a-sum.pdf.

Koppelman, J. 2004. Children with mental disorders: Making sense of their needs and the systems that help them. *National Health Policy Forum,* Issue Brief, no. 799, June 4. Online: www.nhpf.org/pdfs_ib/IB799%5FChildMentalHealth%2Epdf.

Odon, S.L., T. Teferra, & S. Kaul. 2004. An overview of international approaches to early intervention for young children and their families. *Young Children* 59 (5): 38–43.

O'Hagan, K. 1999. Culture, cultural identity, and cultural sensitivity in child and family social work. *Child and Family Social Work* 4: 269–81.

Pipher, M. 2002. *The middle of everywhere: Helping refugees enter the American community.* Orlando, FL: Harcourt.

President's New Freedom Commission on Mental Health. 2003. *Achieving the promise: Transforming mental health care in America.* Final Report. DHHS Pub., no. SMA-03-3832. Rockville, MD: U.S. Department of Health and Human Services. Online: www.mentalhealthcommission.gov.

Triandis, H.C. 1996. The psychological measurement of cultural syndromes. *American Psychologist* 51 (4): 407–15.

U.S. Department of Health and Human Services. 2001. *Mental health: Culture, race, and ethnicity—A supplement to "Mental Health: A Report of the Surgeon General."* Rockville, MD: Public Health Service, Office of the Surgeon General. Online: www.mentalhealth.samhsa.gov/cre/default.asp.

Selected Resources on Culture and Challenging Behavior in Early Childhood Settings

Center for Evidence-Based Practice: Young Children with Challenging Behavior, University of South Florida, is funded by the U.S. Department of Education, Office of Special Education Programs, to increase the awareness and implementation of positive, evidence-based practices and to build an enhanced, accessible database to support those practices. http://challengingbehavior.fmhi.usf.edu/index.html

Center for Social and Emotional Foundations for Early Learning, University of Illinois at Urbana-Champaign, focuses on improving social and emotional outcomes for young children through the provision of resources on evidence-based practice, training materials, and information about state-level strategic planning. Spanish language materials are available. http://csefel.uiuc.edu

Early Childhood Research Institute on Culturally and Linguistically Appropriate Services (CLAS), University of Illinois at Urbana-Champaign, offers resources including practitioner guidelines for the selection of linguistically and culturally appropriate materials and literature reviews of topics in child development and early education. http://clas.uiuc.edu

National Center for Cultural Competence, Georgetown University, has a self-assessment tools checklist that includes some tools designed for professionals providing services in early childhood settings. http://gucchd.georgetown.edu/nccc/selfassessment.html

National Child Care Information Center (NCCIC), Child Care Bureau, Administration for Children and Families, U.S. Department of Health and Human Services, is a clearinghouse for early care and education information for families, providers, policy makers, and researchers. A searchable online library includes Spanish-language resources. http://nccic.org

National Mental Health Information Center, Child and Adolescent Mental Health, U.S. Department of Health and Human Services, Substance Abuse and Mental Health Services Administration (SAMHSA), offers links to campaigns and departments. For resources on culture and mental health, search under "culture, ethnicity, and mental health." www.mentalhealth.samhsa.gov/child/childhealth.asp

Research and Training Center on Family Support and Children's Mental Health, Portland State University, Oregon, conducts collaborative research and disseminates information for families, practitioners, researchers, and policy makers concerned with improving services for children and families with emotional and behavioral disorders. www.rtc.pdx.edu

Recommendations

Here are some recommendations for early childhood professionals to support their practice with families from diverse cultural backgrounds and with children who have disabilities or challenging behaviors.

Learn from families. Be proactive in learning from families, the experts in their culture. Families can share information about their hopes and dreams, goals for their children, and expectations regarding the program and staff. As you interact with families, it is important to be aware of how your own cultural background and professional education and experiences shape your personal values and professional role. Professional knowledge is developed in a cultural context and thus influenced by assumptions about children's behavior that are informed by the dominant cultural view. When you are aware of your own culture and recognize the importance of a family's culture, you are in a better position to provide the individualized services necessary for inclusion. By integrating the family's in-depth knowledge of and goals for their child, you can apply your expertise in a culturally appropriate manner.

© NAEYC

Beware of stereotyping families, and practice a nonjudgmental, unprejudiced attitude. Views of childrearing practices and norms for children's expression and behavior are shaped by culture. Try to remain objective when working with culturally diverse young children with challenging behaviors. The response of parents and professionals to a child's behavior will vary in different cultural contexts. In problem situations, you can reduce the likelihood of culturally based misinterpretation by seeking explanations from the family or from a person well versed in the family's culture. Similarly, consider the family's cultural beliefs and practices when planning ways to remedy situations.

Network with community organizations serving cultural/ethnic groups. Organizations serving particular cultural and ethnic groups exist in many communities. Building networks between early childhood programs and community groups with expertise that is culture-specific is essential in increasing your ability to work effectively with diverse children with disabilities or challenging behaviors and their families. This type of partnership provides access to information about different cultural groups and facilitates connections between families and others who share their culture. In addition, such organizations may be able to provide cultural consultation, for example, to assist an interdisciplinary team engaged in developing specific interventions for a child with behavioral challenges.

Include cultural backgrounds and disabilities in curricula, staff training, and other aspects of the program. To enhance a center's core mission—providing high-quality inclusive care that meets the needs of all children and families—create opportunities to promote respect for differences and increased understanding of different kinds of diversity, including cultural background and disability. This can be done at a number of levels.

For example, *racial/cultural socialization* refers to practices that are unique to an individual, family, or community of a given background and that distinguish the individual, family, or community from other groups in society. Consider integrating culturally specific activities into the center's programming as a way of upholding and celebrating racial and cultural diversity. Invite families to contribute to this process by sharing their cultural knowledge. Be sure to share information with families during planning, so that such activities are done only with the knowledge and approval of all families.

Similarly, examine activities such as staff training or parent education sessions for cultural bias and to ensure that the experiences of families from diverse cultural backgrounds are represented.

Look for commonalities among children and families. Although children's development is rooted in culture, and culture provides an important lens through which to view development, most human beings share similarities in physical, cognitive, and socioemotional development (Greenfield et al. 2003). Look for commonalities among the children and families you serve, and note how such commonalities are shaped and influenced by race, ethnicity, and cultural orientation. Thus, for example, when a child's behavior disrupts the class, consider a range of possible explanations. The meaning of a child's behavior can change over time according to the stage of development. In addition, the meaning of behavior can vary according to the cultural context and individual differences.

Understanding a family's culture is an essential element of your ability to provide inclusive care for diverse children with disabilities or challenging behaviors and their families.

Reading Their Worlds

Working with Diverse Families to Enhance Children's Early Literacy Development

Reading the world always precedes reading the word, and reading the word implies continually reading the world.

— *Paulo Freire and Donaldo Macedo*

**Rosario Ordoñez-Jasis
and Robert W. Ortiz**

SUCCESSFUL, CULTURALLY ENRICHED, AND LINGUISTI-CALLY SENSITIVE family literacy programs incorporate families' life experiences, ways of knowing, educational needs and resources, and goals. Alma Flor Ada (2003) reminds us that "students live in two worlds: home and school. If these two worlds do not recognize, understand, and respect each other, students are put in a difficult predicament" and very little learning can take place (p. 11). As educators working with early childhood educators who want to develop family literacy programs for culturally and linguistically diverse families, we discuss the need for respectful partnerships that build on the strengths of parents and other family members. We encourage educators to begin meaningful two-way conversations that will enable them to read the world of their young students and their families.

Rosario Ordoñez-Jasis, PhD, is an assistant professor in the Reading Department at California State University, Fullerton. Her research and teaching focus on the sociocultural context of literacy and learning in home and school settings. She is the mother of two children, ages five and two.

Robert W. Ortiz, PhD, is a professor in the Special Education Department at California State University, Fullerton. Robert's research interests are in diverse parent involvement in their children's literacy development and bilingual/multicultural special education.

A sociocultural perspective of literacy considers the way parents, children, and extended-family members use literacy at home and in their community. These activities may be initiated by a parent or a child, or they may occur spontaneously as families go about the business of their daily lives. Family literacy programs are usually initiated by outside educational institutions or agencies. The programs are encouraged to build on home literacy practices while supporting the learning and development of school-like literacy behaviors of parents, children, and families (Morrow, Paratore, & Tracey 1994).

Brazilian educator Paulo Freire states that learning to read the written word is intertwined with the knowledge and meaning that is derived from reading one's world (Freire & Macedo 1987). Reading the world, according to Freire, includes understanding how our lives are shaped by complex and multifaceted sociocultural factors—our cultural identity, family history, employment, education, community, and long-term (individual and collective) goals and dreams (Compton-Lily 2003). These emerging understandings influence how we interpret and interact with text, which in turn greatly influences how we learn to reread or decode our worlds and everyday realities.

When creating comprehensive and culturally relevant family literacy programs, educators need to try to read the worlds of the children they teach and their families. As teachers talk with families in order to understand their lives outside of school, not only do they gain a better sense of families' sociocultural contexts, but they also validate a wealth of stories, dispositions, motivations, and cultural information or "funds of knowledge" (Moll & Gonzalez 2004) that become the building blocks for a comprehensive family literacy program.

Beyond a deficit paradigm

The importance of parent involvement in children's education is well documented. Family involvement is associated with children's higher test scores, better attendance and behavior, and stronger cognitive skills (Darling 1992). Research on parent involvement in early literacy development shows that early reading experiences prepare children for the benefits of formal literacy instruction and build a foundation for later reading success (Burns, Griffin, & Snow 1999).

Auerbach (1995) argues that current approaches to family literacy programs, particularly those targeted toward families with low incomes and families from diverse cultural backgrounds, tend to take a neodeficit approach. That is, despite the recent discourse on the need to build on family strengths (Nieto 2002; Riojas-Cortez, Flores, & Clark 2003), many educational programs fail to fully recognize, incorporate, or tap into the wealth of literacy information, skills, and knowledge parents may hold. Despite evidence to the contrary (Moll & Gonzalez 2004; Ordoñez-Jasis & Jasis 2004; Ortiz 1998), culturally and linguistically diverse parents are too often viewed as not supporting their children's school success (Darling 1992; Volk & Long 2005). In addition, the ways in which such families involve themselves in their children's schooling often go unrecognized by school staff (Lareau 1994).

Culturally and linguistically diverse parents value literacy and see it as the single most powerful hope for their children's future.

Parent early literacy involvement calls for a renewed understanding and acknowlegment of the depth and diversity of home-based knowledge as children begin to acquire formal literacy skills (Darling 1992; Ortiz & Ordoñez-Jasis 2005; Volk & Long 2005). Many culturally and linguistically diverse parents value literacy and see it as the single most powerful hope for their children's future (Flores, Cousin, & Diaz 1998; Nieto 2002).

Basics for a Family Survey

These questions may serve as a starting point in developing family literacy curricula based on family members' background information:

- If recently arrived in the United States, what is the family's country of origin?
- In what language do the adult family members prefer to read?
- What interests does the family have?
- What types of reading material do both parents enjoy?
- How comfortable are the parents and other family members in reading to the children?
- What are their goals for sharing literacy activities with their children?

Teachers may need the assistance of an interpreter for families who are learning English. They can use the information collected to incorporate fun, interesting, and meaningful reading activities in home and school experiences.

© Elisabeth Nichols

Recommendations for family literacy initiatives

Early childhood educators can have a greater impact on children's literacy development when they view parents as providers of information as well as recipients. As teachers begin to embrace both the words and the worlds of parents, they learn to assist and broaden the role of families in their children's literacy learning and establish home-school relationships based on mutual respect and trust.

To promote culturally sensitive family literacy programs, we offer the following recommendations.

Reflect on individual and program views about family involvement.

Although educators say they support parent involvement, the approach to family literacy used by many schools and individual teachers is based on deficit assumptions that marginalize parent voices and efforts (Darling 1992; Lareau 1994). For example, many programs choose books that reflect mainstream values and lifestyles rather than considering families' cultures. Staff's in-depth discussions and examination of a program's family involvement policies are an important first step toward improving the program's efforts (Ada, Campoy, & Zubizarreta 2001). During this process, teachers should also reflect individually on

© Janice Bell

their own personal dispositions and their assumptions and expectations about the involvement of parents from minority groups, in particular. For example, Flores, Cousin, and Diaz describe the need for educators to identify what they refer to as "habitually

unexamined attitudes" (1998, 27) that consciously and unconsciously impact how we interact with diverse children and their families. With these renewed understandings, educators can outline their program's goals and content related to family literacy agendas, objectively assess the program's strengths and weaknesses, and make the necessary changes.

Ask both parents to share information about their literacy backgrounds.

Family surveys, individual interviews, focus groups, and home observations can provide a wealth of information about family situations and parent perceptions and expectations of the functions of literacy in their lives (see "Basics for a Family Survey," p. 45).

Offer diverse reading material.

Families tend to choose reading material that is interesting, helpful, and important to them. Try to include authentic multicultural literature that reflects the rich, diverse realities of families. The following themes are relevant to many families: preserving tradition, celebrating the richness of culture and family life, telling one's personal story, telling stories of people who share similar experiences,

As teachers begin to embrace both the words and the worlds of parents, they learn to **assist and broaden the role of families** in their children's literacy learning.

When sharing literary selections with families, offer a variety of genres in the parents' language of preference.

© Marilyn Nolt

and addressing social issues and concerns (Ada 2003). When sharing literary selections with families, educators should offer a variety of genres: poetry, drama, biography, autobiography, history, and contemporary fiction and fantasy in the parents' language of preference. Literature should also reflect the culture of the family, thus supporting the idea that their ethnic background is respected and an integral part of the children's learning process (Nieto 2002; Moll & Gonzalez 2004; Ortiz & Ordoñez-Jasis 2005). Parents can help schools identify appropriate reading materials while educators, in turn, can seek out texts to share with parents.

Use the parents' primary language.

"Language is one of the strongest elements in one's self-definition as an individual and a social being" (Ada 2003, 7). Paying attention to the home language raises it to a place of dignity and respect while allowing parents to show their reading and writing skills in the language they feel most comfortable using. Although some parents may lack the English skills needed for high-level conversations and preliteracy activities, many have a rich home language foundation to support critical parent-child interactions (Tabors & Snow 2002).

Provide children's reading material in the family's home language and encourage adults to read to their children in that language. When appropriate, send home translated materials for special events, such as invitations for workshops, event reminders, preworkshop interest surveys, and program descriptions. Conduct parent workshops and conferences in the parents' primary language. Studies reveal the many positive outcomes of using families' primary languages in family literacy workshops (Delgado-Gaitan 1990; Riojas-Cortez, Flores, & Clark 2003; Moll & Gonzalez 2004). When this is not possible, provide a translator, drawing upon the rich linguistic resources of potential parent liaisons within schools.

Consider the role of parents who are not able to read or write.

Parents who cannot read or write fluently in either their primary language or in English still play a critical role in their child's literacy learning. Communicate to all parents the importance of oral language, because it is a strong precursor to early literacy development (Burns, Griffin, & Snow 1999). Children's dramatic and creative expressions are enhanced when parents engage children in rhymes, songs, riddles, oral history, poetry, proverbs, and folklore (Ada 2003).

Educators can encourage all parents to engage their children in enriching dialogue and language play. Through storytelling, for example, parents can create their own story with a beginning, middle, and end. This helps prepare children to understand the complex components of literacy, such as phonemic awareness, vocabulary development, and comprehension (Isbell 2002), as well as literary features such as motive for action, author/audience relationships, and the cultural definitions of a good story (Craig et al. 2001).

Teachers can model how to use wordless picture books to teach children important early literacy skills such as predicting, story sequencing, concepts of print, describing details within illustrations, and identifying key story elements or main characters. Wordless picture books are excellent tools for helping children and parents appreciate the aesthetic pleasures of books while developing creativity and imagination.

Offer a variety of approaches to connect with parents.

For numerous reasons, some parents may not involve themselves in their children's schooling (Lareau 1994; Burningham & Dever 2005). Some parents may work two or more jobs, making it difficult for them to attend school functions. Others may rely on public transportation. Recent immigrant parents may be hesitant to attend school activities because they are unfamiliar with the U.S. educational system, or they may feel that they do not understand or speak English well enough to talk with their child's teacher. Other parents may have had negative experiences when they themselves were students in U.S. schools and consequently distrust school officials. For parents such as these, it is particularly important to create common ground and avoid making negative assumptions about their educational values and expectations (Nieto 2002).

Teachers can attempt a variety of approaches to connect with parents. They should be flexible in scheduling and vary the times when workshops are offered throughout the year. They can consider providing child care services for parents who would not otherwise be able to attend.

Tailor the program for families with children who have special needs.

For parents whose children have special needs, it is important to pay attention to the child's learning needs and how they affect the acquisition of specific reading and writing skills, such as letter recognition, word comprehension, and pronunciation. Children with disabilities face great risks in relation to literacy development when their parents hold low expectations for the children's success (Light & Kelford-Smith 1993).

> Wordless picture books are excellent tools for helping children and parents **appreciate the aesthetic pleasures of books** while developing creativity and imagination.

It is recommended that school personnel collaborate with parents and plan ways to foster children's literacy learning. Although academic learning concerns are addressed during Individualized Education Plan (IEP) meetings at the school, staff should encourage parents to meet with teachers during the school year and also to learn about strategies they can use at home to support their children's reading and writing skills. Educators should provide information for families on ways to minimize the effects of the disability on the child's development while at the same time building a positive parent-child relationship. With a full understanding of the impact of a disability on the learning process, parent involvement can be a meaningful experience—for both parent and child.

Envision literacy as a means to empower families.

There is a critical link between literacy, self-development, and empowerment, because literacy enables transformative thought and social action (Freire & Macedo 1987; Volk & Long 2005). Delgado-Gaitan's (1990) and Jasis's (2000) research with Latino families, for example, shows how schools and literacy programs can play a role in establishing parent networks that can make decisions that improve schooling. Literacy as a social and transformative act can help families—both individually and collectively—understand and change their social conditions (Delgado-Gaitan 1990). Parent training sessions can begin with a safe space: a place to reflect and share stories of triumphs, frustrations, and lessons learned about their literacy experiences as children and adults both in and out of school. This practice can help build a community of learners. It establishes common ground whereby parents develop agency and gain the confidence to coconstruct new learning-based literacy activities with their children (Jasis & Ordoñez-Jasis 2005).

> There is a **critical link** between literacy, self-development, and empowerment.

CLEMENTINA'S CACTUS
EZRA JACK KEATS

Changes, Changes
By PAT HUTCHINS

The Snowman
RAYMOND BRIGGS

Have You Seen My Duckling?
Nancy Tafuri

GOOD NIGHT, GORILLA
Peggy Rathmann

Conclusion

Family literacy programs can lead to long-lasting, positive results when they encourage parents and other family members to reflect critically on their relationships with their children and to think about the role of literacy in their lives. As parents increase their sense of belonging and responsibility, and possibly learn to reread their world in new and exciting ways (Freire & Macedo 1987), they can begin to share in the empowering experience of creating a better place for their children via literacy activities.

© Elisabeth Nichols

Parent involvement in children's early literacy experiences can enhance children's academic achievement. And while families differ in their experiences and literacy practices, as well as in their understanding of learning processes, reading and doing related activities together seem to strengthen children's abilities to decode and interpret their world. Through early exposure to literacy practices, children become increasingly equipped to enter a literary world that is filled with wonder and adventure.

Many parents engage in daily literacy activities with their children, although they may not be fully aware of the educational impact of their involvement. But when mothers, fathers, and other family members share print and text with a child, they can become valuable resources and meaning makers in their children's lives. Culturally enriched and linguistically sensitive family literacy programs can strengthen and expand these powerful parent-child dynamics. Family literacy programs and initiatives have a greater chance of long-term success and effectiveness when they tap into families' readings of the world around them (Moll & Gonzalez 2004). When dialogue and interaction between home and school are based on a more equal exchange of knowledge, it leads to an appreciation for and understanding of each by the other. Society and schools are enriched by the diversity produced through this interactive dialogue.

References

Ada, A.F. 2003. *A magical encounter: Latino children's literature in the classroom.* Boston: Allyn & Bacon.

Ada, A.F., F.I. Campoy, & R. Zubizarreta. 2001. Assessing our work with parents on behalf of children's literacy. In *Literacy assessment of second language learners,* eds. S. Hurley & J. Tinajero, 167–85.

Auerbach, E. 1995. Deconstructing the discourse of strengths in family literacy. *Journal of Reading Behavior* 27: 643–61.

Burningham, L., & M.T. Dever. 2005. An interactive model for fostering family literacy. *Young Children* 60 (5): 87–94.

Burns, M.S., P. Griffin, & C.E. Snow, eds. 1999. *Starting out right: A guide to promoting children's reading success.* Washington, DC: National Academy Press. Online: www.nap.edu/html/gov.

Compton-Lily, L. 2003. *Reading families: The literate lives of urban children.* New York: Teachers College Press.

Craig, S., K. Hull, A.G. Haggart, & E. Crowder. 2001. Storytelling: Addressing the literacy needs of diverse learners. *Teaching Exceptional Children* 33 (5): 46–51.

Darling, S. 1992. Family literacy: Parents and children learning together. *Principal* 72 (2): 10–12.

Delgado-Gaitan, C. 1990. *Literacy for empowerment: The role of parents in children's education.* London: Falmer.

Flores, B., T.C. Cousin, & E. Diaz. 1998. Transforming deficit myths about learning, language, and culture. In *Literacy instruction for culturally and linguistically diverse students,* ed. M.F. Opitz, 27–38. Newark, DE: International Reading Association.

Freire, P., & D. Macedo. 1987. *Literacy: Reading the world and the word.* Westport, CT: Bergin & Garvey.

Isbell, R. 2002. Telling and retelling stories: Learning language and literacy. *Young Children* 57 (2): 27–30.

Jasis, P. 2000. Building La Familia: Organization and empowerment with Latino parents in a public school. Dissertation, University of California, Berkeley.

Jasis, P., & R. Ordoñez-Jasis. 2005. *Convivencia* to empowerment: Latino parent organizing at La Familia. *The High School Journal* 88 (2): 32–42.

Lareau, A. 1994. Parent involvement in schooling: A dissenting view. In *School, family and community interaction,* eds. C. Fagnano & B. Werber, 61–73. San Francisco: Westview.

Light, J., & A. Kelford-Smith. 1993. The home literacy experiences of preschoolers who use augmentative communication systems and of their nondisabled peers. *Augmentative and Alternative Communication* 9 (1): 10–25.

Moll, L., & N. Gonzalez. 2004. Beginning where children are. In *Tongue-tied: The lives of multilingual children in public education,* ed. O. Santa Ana, 152–56. Lanham, MD: Rowman & Littlefield.

Morrow, L.M., J.R. Paratore, & D.H. Tracey. 1994. *Family literacy: New perspectives, new opportunities.* Newark, DE: International Reading Association.

Nieto, S. 2002. *Language, culture, and teaching: Critical perspectives for a new century.* Mahwah, NJ: Erlbaum.

Ordoñez-Jasis, R., & P. Jasis. 2004. Rising with De Colores: Tapping into the resources of *la comunidad* to assist under-performing Chicano/Latino students. *Journal of Latinos and Education* 1 (4): 53–64.

Ortiz, R.W. 1998. Chipping away at the monolith: Dispelling the myth of father noninvolvement in children's early literacy development. *Family Preservation Journal* 3 (2): 73–94.

Ortiz, R.W., & R. Ordoñez-Jasis. 2005. *Leyendo Juntos*—Reading together: New directions for Latino parent early literacy involvement. *Reading Teacher* 59 (2): 110–21.

Riojas-Cortez, M., B. Flores, & E. Clark. 2003. *Los niños aprenden en casa:* Valuing and connecting home cultural knowledge with an early childhood program. *Young Children* 58 (6): 78–83.

Tabors, P., & C. Snow. 2002. Young bilingual children and literacy development. In *Handbook of early literacy research,* eds. S.B. Neuman & D.K. Dickson, 159–78. New York: Guilford.

Volk, D., & S. Long. 2005. Challenging myths of the deficit perspective: Honoring children's literacy resources. *Young Children* 60 (6): 12–19.

Leave No Parent Behind

Three Proven Strategies

© Ellen B. Senisi

Many families of preschoolers are eager to support their young learners both inside and outside the classroom. To do this effectively, families must know what skills their children need to be successful in kindergarten and beyond. Families also need to learn specific strategies for reinforcing math, literacy, social studies, science, and other kinds of learning in developmentally appropriate ways.

Increasingly, early childhood programs are stepping in to educate families about the expectations of their local school system and to provide family-friendly activities that promote and reinforce children's learning. Three such programs are described in the following brief articles (pp. 50–54). For further information, readers can contact the authors at the e-mail addresses provided.

Leaps and Bounds

Preparing Parents for Kindergarten

Michelle Rhodes, Billie Enz, and Marilyn LaCount

RESEARCH STUDIES CONDUCTED OVER THE PAST 25 YEARS consistently demonstrate that children whose families help them prepare for school by engaging in reading, math, and social activities are highly successful in school (Henderson & Berla 1994; Snow, Burns, & Griffin 1998; Ramey & Ramey 1999). Promoting school readiness by strengthening partnerships with families is a complex but worthy task. When schools acknowledge the relevance of children's home cultures and promote parent involvement, they can develop a supportive environment for learning through meaningful activities that engage and empower families (Snow, Burns, & Griffin 1998; Ramey & Ramey 1999).

The Office of Youth Preparation, in partnership with Arizona State University's Department of Early Childhood Education and New Directions Institute for Infant Brain Development, created Leaps and Bounds: A Kindergarten Readiness Program to provide education and support to families underserved by other agencies in the Phoenix metropolitan area. This research-based program provides practical knowledge on helping children prepare for kindergarten to a community primarily comprising Spanish-speaking parents with low incomes. The family-friendly activities included in the program use items found in the home to promote three learning areas: logico-mathematic knowledge, language-literacy development, and social competence (see "Around the House/ *En la casa*" as an example). The activities align with the Arizona Early Childhood and Kindergarten Readiness Standards.

Leaps and Bounds includes four 75-minute-long workshops held at times convenient for families over a one-month time period. The workshops are intended to help parents become more aware of everyday opportunities for learning. Activities and materials are presented in both English and Spanish to support the home language used by the target population.

Michelle Rhodes, MS, is a doctoral candidate in Arizona State University's (ASU) College of Education, Division of Curriculum and Instruction, early childhood education program area. She is program director for Leaps and Bounds and a faculty associate for the College of Education.

Billie J. Enz, PhD, associate director for the Division of Curriculum and Instruction in the College of Education at ASU, has developed many school-family partnership initiatives in the state of Arizona, the Navajo Nation, and Mexico.

Marilyn R. LaCount, MEd, is director of the Office of Youth Preparation and former director of Leaps and Bounds at ASU. She provides administrative oversight for the implementation of a variety of pre-K–12 outreach programs and initiatives at school sites and in the community.

Activities for 3 year olds & beyond

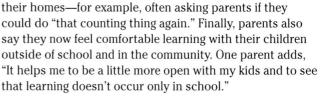

Around the House

En La Casa

Why it is important!

Drawing and measuring activities provide the opportunities for children to learn dexterity, fine motor control and eye-hand coordination. These types of activities also increase opportunities for meaningful language experiences and early mathematical thinking.

Activity #2
How Many Hands?

Materials Needed: Your hands and different sized, shaped items around the house to be used for measuring.

1. Use different sized and shaped items to have your child find the length and height of furniture or other things in your living room.

2. Help your child make guesses, compare and talk about different sizes and shapes.

3. See if there is a difference when you use your hands to measure the same things.

Relates to AZ Readiness Standards: 2M-R1, 2M-R2, 5M-R1, 5M-R2, 6M-R1

Relates to AZ ECD Standards: SED 2.1; PD1.3; LL1.2, 1.3; M 1.1,3.1, 5.1; SC 1.1

Actividades para niños de 3 o más años

¡Porqué es importante!

Las actividades de medir y dibujar cosas ofrecen una oportunidad a niños para aprender destrezas, el control de los músculos y la coordinación. Esta clase de actividad también aumenta las oportunidades para experiencias significativas de lenguaje y de análisis matemático.

Actividad #2
¿Cuántas Manos?

Materiales Necesarios: Sus manos y objetos de la casa de diferentes tamaños y formas que se van a usar para medir.

1. Pida a su niño(a) que use los objetos de la casa de diferentes tamaños y formas para medir la altitud y longitud de muebles y otras cosas en su sala.

2. Ayude a que su hijo(a) adivine, discuta y compare diferentes tamaños y formas.

3. Note si hay alguna diferencia cuando usa sus manos para medir las mismas cosas.

Relacionado con 'Arizona Readiness Standards': 2M-R1, 2M-R2, 5M-R1, 5M-R2, 6M-R1

Relacionado con 'Arizona Readiness Standards': SED 2.1; PD1.3; LL1.2, 1.3; M 1.1,3.1, 5.1; SC 1.1

During the workshops, teachers demonstrate learning activities that parents and children can replicate at home. Facilitators explain briefly how each activity promotes learning. After parents and children participate in hands-on activities, facilitators brainstorm with family members to help them think of ways to extend these activities further in their homes.

Program staff used follow-up questionnaires and phone interviews to determine the effectiveness of the workshops. Early results indicate that families are spending an average of one to three additional hours per week doing the activities modeled in the workshops. Parents comment that they feel "more important" and "empowered" to act as their child's first teacher.

Most interesting is the fact that families report that their children initiate the events in

© Ellen B. Senisi

their homes—for example, often asking parents if they could do "that counting thing again." Finally, parents also say they now feel comfortable learning with their children outside of school and in the community. One parent adds, "It helps me to be a little more open with my kids and to see that learning doesn't occur only in school."

The Leaps and Bounds program has been a success. By providing parents and family members with knowledge, demonstrations, and support, the program encourages them to spend more time engaging their children in learning activities. Programs like Leaps and Bounds help parents use inexpensive and immediately accessible resources to prepare their children for kindergarten.

References

Henderson, A.T., & N. Berla. 1994. *A new generation of evidence: The family is critical to student achievement.* Washington, DC: National Committee for Citizens in Education. ERIC ED 375968.

Ramey, C.T., & S.L. Ramey. 1999. Beginning school for children at risk. In *The transition to kindergarten,* eds. R.C. Pianta & M.J. Cox, 217–52. Baltimore: Brookes.

Snow, C., S. Burns, & P. Griffin. 1998. *Preventing reading difficulties in young children.* Washington, DC: National Academies Press.

For more information about the Leaps and Bounds program, e-mail **LeapsandBounds@asu.edu**.

Home Connections to Learning
Supporting Parents as Teachers

Yvette Mass and Kathleen Ann Cohan

Carlos Martinez raced down the hall ahead of his mother. "I saw you on TV last night, Ms. Cohan," Carlos said as his teacher greeted him. "And I even saw me!" Mrs. Martinez, seconds behind, explained, "Right after dinner we played the video. We watched it three times, and Carlos couldn't wait to do the activity packets. He did them all in one night because he was so excited. And when he got stuck, I knew just how to help him because I saw what you did in the video." Ms. Cohan smiled and joined in the conversation. She was pleased to hear that the lending library was a success.

BUSY WITH WORK AND OTHER RESPON-SIBILITIES, families with low incomes sometimes have difficulty finding the time to engage their preschoolers in the kinds of stimulating conversations and spontaneous learning experiences that build rich background knowledge and basic skills. To complicate this situation, many of the parents of children enrolled in our program have limited math and literacy skills, and 35 percent of the families are nonnative English speakers. As a result, some of the parents of the children in our Head Start and pre-K programs may need guidance in what they can do to help their children acquire the skills needed for kindergarten, such as recognizing the letters in their own name, counting, matching, and identifying colors.

To support parents as their child's first teacher, the academic support staff and Head Start and pre-K teachers developed Home Connections to Learning, a strategy designed to help families learn ways to help their children build foundational skills at home. The strategy includes a series of teacher-led math and literacy lessons that were videotaped and used to establish a lending library. The

tapes demonstrate ways teachers guide and instruct children in learning literacy and math skills and serve as a model for parents to use at home to support their children's learning.

Each videotape begins with an introduction by the teacher, stating the focus of the lesson. This gives parents a clear understanding of the skills to be presented. On each tape the teacher begins by reading aloud while encouraging children to interact with the text, inviting them to locate pictures, letters, and shapes. Following the read-aloud, children engage in hands-on activities to reinforce the focus of the lesson. The tapes also show strategies teachers use to determine how well children understand the lesson.

In addition, teachers developed follow-up activities that support and/or extend the skills presented in each video-tape. Each packet provided to families includes the videotape as well as books, games, and hands-on activities for parents and children to play together to reinforce the skills shared on the tape.

We held two meetings with families—one to present the program and a second to obtain feedback about their experiences. The overall response was very positive. Parents enjoyed seeing their child on videotape and had a better understanding of the learning that occurred in the classroom. Many parents felt the program helped their child gain English-language skills, and several parents

Yvette Mass, MS, is a media productions teacher in the Humanities and Communication Magnet Program at Eastern Middle School in Silver Spring, Maryland. She has collaborated with teachers on technology integration and developed technology projects that enhance student learning.

Kathleen Cohan, MS, teaches kindergarten at Beall Elementary School in Rockville, Maryland. Her 20 years teaching experience includes four years as a Head Start teacher. She is a candidate for National Board Certification in Early/Middle Childhood Literacy.

Photos courtesy of the authors.

commented that it helped them improve their own English skills as well. One parent noted, "After watching Mrs. Liebow ask questions as she read the book, I now ask questions. I don't just read the book to my child."

Similarly, parents stated they had a better understanding of how to help their child build math and literacy skills. Another parent, who was worried that her child did not participate in class, was pleased to see her daughter actively involved in the lessons. All of the parents noted that their children enjoyed seeing or hearing themselves in the video. Many children asked to see the video several times.

As a result of the discussion at the second family meeting, teachers became aware of the ways literacy skills differ in various cultures. For instance, Chinese-speaking parents informed teachers that the concept of rhyming words does not exist in their language. Parents also said the activity packets reflected the school district's high expectations for math and literacy skills as well as learning behaviors for pre-schoolers. Parents realized that they need to encourage their child to stay focused and to persist in completing a task.

This program helped children develop a foundation in math and literacy skills because they received additional targeted support at home. We hope that Home Connections to Learning laid the groundwork for parents in guiding their children's early learning experiences and will help them continue collaborative partnerships with the school that can result in their children being well-prepared, confident, and successful students.

For more information about Home Connections to Learning, contact Kathleen_A_Cohan@mcpsmd.org or Yvette_Mass@mcpsmd.org.

Virtual Pre-K
Connecting Home, School, and Community

Alicia Narvaez, Jessica Feldman, and Christopher Theriot

EARLY CHILDHOOD PROFESSIONALS have long known that involved families have an enormous impact on a child's early learning. We also know that teachers are constantly looking for creative and developmentally appropriate ways to engage parents in the learning process. School administrators are seeking effective and economical family involvement programs. Most parents want to be involved; they just need a little support to make it happen. So, how do we get there?

Enter Virtual Pre-K, a Chicago Public Schools (CPS) program developed by active master teachers with decades of classroom experience. Virtual Pre-K is an interactive educational resource in English and Spanish that bridges classroom learning with hands-on home activities and community experiences. Short video clips, 10 on each of the two videos described below, demonstrate each activity, giving a realistic model of best practices for teachers and parents. There are activity recipe cards for parents and lesson plans for teachers with step-by-step instructions, a list of the easily found materials needed to do each activity, and recommended books. An interactive Web site with a community calendar takes the learning online (**www.virtualpre-k.org**) and complements any early childhood curriculum. Coordinated teaching and learning make teachers and parents true partners in early education and build parents' confidence by demonstrating that they already possess the skills and materials to help their children learn at home.

CPS launched the first Virtual Pre-K program called *All About Me* in October 2001, covering themes of self-discovery, feelings, and one's place in the world. Next came *Taking Care of Me* in 2002, focusing on themes of nutrition, health, and safety. Each video integrates early literacy with math, science, and social studies. The program is low cost, fun, and easy. Says one parent, "There are things that don't cost much that you have around the house, and from these you can do an activity."

Experience a sample lesson

Let's step into a Chicago classroom and experience a Virtual Pre-K lesson called "Giving Words Meaning."

"Caps for sale! Fifty cents a cap!" Jessica parades around the classroom with a stack of brightly decorated newspaper hats piled high atop her head. Jessica is

Alicia Narvaez, MPA, is director of the Virtual Pre-K and Virtual Kindergarten programs for the Chicago public schools. Alicia works with districts and educational agencies nationwide to adapt and implement Virtual Pre-K across a wide variety of early childhood programs.

Jessica Feldman, MPP, is a graduate student in the University of Chicago Department of Sociology. She worked as an intern for the Virtual Pre-K program, conducting a comprehensive program evaluation and leading parent-training workshops.

Christopher Theriot, MPP, assists with the marketing and expansion of Virtual Pre-K to other school districts. He came to the Chicago public schools as a grant developer and has also worked in the New Schools Development Department.

Photos courtesy of the authors

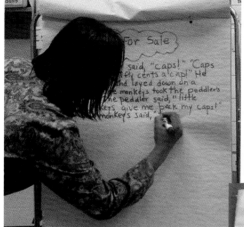

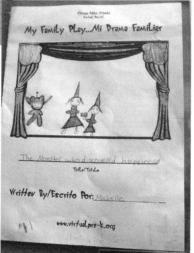

playing the role of the peddler in Esphyr Slobodkina's *Caps for Sale,* a much-loved story she and her classmates are reading. Using recycled newspapers, feathers, buttons, and paint, the children created their own hats earlier in the week. As a group, the children decided who would play each role as they acted out the story. When it comes time for the peddler to recover her caps, Jessica stamps her foot and shakes her finger, saying, "You monkeys you, give me back my caps!" As the monkeys imitate Jessica's movement, the children burst into laughter.

For the at-home activity, the child dictates a story from her imagination while a parent or sibling writes it down. Then the family can act out the story together. The home activity reinforces the classroom learning and links the class and home in an exciting new way. "I'm like a little kid all over again," comments one working mom. "At the same time that you join in the activities, you're helping the kids and they're learning too." By taking part in shared learning experiences with their child, parents engage in their natural role as teachers, sometimes without even realizing it.

Some parents carry the lesson even further by attending a chil-dren's theater production as part of the out-and-about community connection. This widens the scope of parent involvement even further.

Virtual Pre-K goes national

When we launched Virtual Pre-K in Chicago, we never dreamed we'd be partnering with other school districts to share our program across the country. When we presented Virtual Pre-K at conferences, educators kept asking, "How can we bring Virtual Pre-K to *our* schools?"

Through the Virtual Pre-K National Network, school districts and educational agencies join a growing collaboration of educators and families committed to strengthening the home-school partnership in early childhood education.

For more information about Virtual Pre-K and the National Network, visit **www. virtualpre-k.org** or contact the author at **anarvaez@virtualpre-k.org.**

Family Involvement in an International School

Piloting a Parent-Teacher Reading Group

Gail Wentworth

THE INTERNATIONAL SCHOOL OF GENEVA is an exciting multinational environment, and it proved to be an excellent setting in which to start a parent-teacher reading group. The project's main purpose was to develop positive relationships with families from a wide array of cultures. The reading group model is a strategy early childhood professionals can use for developing partnerships with families in most any context.

An early childhood experience abroad

While living in Switzerland, I taught preschool and was the early childhood coordinator at the Pregny-Rigot campus of the International School. The 22 four-year-olds in the preschool class were from Europe, Asia, Africa, North America, South America, and Australia. They spoke 10 different mother tongues. The Swiss teaching assistant spoke French to the children and I spoke English, as was the model in each classroom. We were very creative and fairly successful in using a variety of verbal and nonverbal methods to communicate with the children and their families.

The diplomatic and international nature of many parents' jobs entailed frequent moves. This meant that new children were enrolling in the early childhood program throughout the year. Some parents spoke limited English and/or French; some came from countries with very different philosophies of education for young children; and

Gail E. Wentworth, EdD, is associate professor of early childhood at State University of New York in Cobleskill. Gail has worked with children and families in Europe and the United States. She is currently piloting a family-staff reading group in Cobleskill.

Photos courtesy of the author

most were experiencing the stress associated with relocation and culture shock (Weaver 2000).

Families' concerns

The families of the preschoolers asked me numerous questions about young children's development and appropriate educational practices. I found myself frequently explaining developmentally appropriate practice (Bredekamp & Copple 1997) and the school's adopted curriculum, "Primary Years Programme in the Early Childhood Years" (IBO 2000; Wentworth 2003). Occasionally I defended my teaching practices to parents whose experiences with schooling for young children were quite different. This was especially the case among some of the Asian families, who were used to a standards-centered versus a child-centered curriculum. Families expressed concern because when they returned to their home countries, their children would be expected to function in a much more structured learning environment. They worried that their children would not be able to keep up with the class. I also realized that some parents I talked with were craving connection to a community and relished the time they spent chatting and hanging out in the classroom after school.

> Some parents enjoyed lingering in my classroom after school . . . I realized they were **craving connection to a community** and relished chatting and hanging out in the classroom after school.

After a year of fielding parents' questions, chatting at length with parents after school, and distributing readings to address parental concerns, I decided to start a monthly reading group.

A reading group is born

The parent-teacher reading group was a collaborative learning situation comprising a small but dedicated multi-cultural group of adults from the children's lives: family members, caregivers, and educators. Here's how it worked.

Linda Kwon, the five-year-olds teacher, and I asked interested participants to suggest topics for reading and discussion. I perused professional resources for relevant articles in English. We made copies of the selected article available for anyone who wanted to come to the meeting or just read on their own. It was exciting to note that a diverse group asked for readings and came to at least one of our meetings—mothers, one father, teachers, nannies and au pairs, teaching assistants, special education assistants, and school administrators.

The group met in the preschool classroom once a month for about an hour and a half in the early evening. On a tablecloth spread on one of the children's tables we set crackers, cheese, grapes, spring water, and wine (remember, this was Europe!). People socialized for a bit before embarking on a discussion of the month's reading. First we discussed the reading in pairs, and then we got together as a group to share our thoughts.

Gratifying results

The reading group provided a forum for educators to talk about their early childhood philosophies and teaching strategies in a relaxed setting. Parents and educators

Tips for Starting a Parent-Teacher Reading Group

The reading group model could be adapted to any early childhood setting. Here are some suggestions for parents and educators interested in starting a group.

• Ask parents about the most convenient times for them to meet.

• Offer snacks and child care.

• Let parents lead the discussion—more talk from them, less from you!

• Practice respectful listening and welcome all points of view.

• Let people know that they are welcome to partici-pate in one, some, or all meetings.

• Give no homework! (Except the monthly reading)

• Encourage people to read even if they can't attend the meeting.

• Follow up with a newsletter to share the highlights of each month's discussion.

• Look for ways to get more men involved.

getting to know one another and sharing stories about their children and their own childhoods was, to Linda and me, the most valuable outcome for the group. People left smiling and chatting with new acquaintances.

As often happens when people from various cultures come together willingly, a new understanding of similari-ties and differences emerged. For example, I found that my own second-generation Italian American upbringing near Boston was more similar to a Sri Lankan parent's upbring-ing than to an American colleague's. Moments like this, when we recognize something we hold in common, are wonderful for opening deeper levels of communication and understanding. As far as developing community, mission accomplished!

In addition to making connections and discov-ering commonalities in our cultures, we dis-cussed early childhood growth and learning, developmen-tally appropriate teaching practices, and curricula. The group functioned as a community of learners, and our new

> Moments in which we **recognize commonalities** create deeper levels of communication and understanding.

understandings strengthened the overall quality of the early childhood program. Looking back, I believe the parent-teacher reading group was a real success.

References

Bredekamp, S., & C. Copple, eds. 1997. *Developmentally appropriate practice in early childhood programs.* Rev. ed. Washington, DC: NAEYC.

Gestwicki, C. 2004. *Home, school, and community relations.* New York: Delmar.

IBO (International Baccalaureate Organisation). 2000. *The Primary Years Programme in the early childhood years (3–5 years).* Geneva, Switzerland: Author.

Weaver, G.P. 2000. *Culture, communication, and conflict.* 2nd ed. Boston: Pearson.

Wentworth, G.E. 2003. *Pregny-Rigot Early Childhood Program guide.* Geneva, Switzerland: International School of Geneva, Pregny-Rigot Campus.

Parent-Teacher Reading Group—A Success!

Dear Families,

The first meeting of the parent-teacher reading group was a success. After some light food and drink, we sat down together to discuss commercialism and the media and their effects on young children. It was great to get both parents' and teachers' perspectives. We voiced concerns and shared some ideas to help children develop a critical eye for television and commercials for toys or foods directly marketed to them. We'd like to share two practical strategies that some parents use to help their children with these issues.

Some families ask their children to first choose something to give away before they purchase something new. For example, if a child wants a new doll that she sees in a store, she has to go home and look among the dolls she already has, and choose one to donate to another child before purchasing the new one. This is a great idea! The child must stop and think about how much she really wants the new toy. Sometimes the result is that the child is not ready to part with a toy, and so decides she doesn't want to buy anything. There's a real lesson for the child!

Here's another idea that a mother shared. Before going out to the shops, the parents talk to their young children about what they will likely see (stores with toys, sweets, etc.) They make it clear to the children that they will not be buying anything. The children can, however, *look* at things that interest them. What a wonderful idea! The parents make looking at attractive toys a special treat. In fact, their older son typically asks, "Mommy, there's that new action figure! Can I go and look at it?" There is no discussion about purchasing the toy because that issue was made clear before they left the house! Try making *looking* a privilege for your children.

At our next meeting we'll discuss aspects of children's development related to gender and racial awareness. Please join us! Ask your child's teacher for our new reading.

Most Sincerely,

Gail Wentworth and Linda Kwon

Resources for Supporting and Involving Families in Meaningful Ways

Young Children articles and NAEYC books

Baker, A., & L. Manfredi/Pettit. 2004. *Relationships, the heart of quality care: Creating community among adults in early care settings.* Washington, DC: NAEYC.

Balaban, N. 2005. *Everyday goodbyes: Starting school and early care: A guide to the separation process.* New York: Teachers College Press. Available from NAEYC.

Birckmayer, J., J. Cohen, I.D. Jansen, & D.A. Variano. 2005. Kyle lives with his granny—Where are his mommy and daddy? Supporting grandparents who raise grandchildren. *Young Children* 60 (3): 100–04.

Briody, J. 2005. Family Ties. Separation through a parent's eyes. *Young Children* 60 (2): 110–11.

Buell, M.J., R.A. Hallam, & H.L. Beck. 2001. Early Head Start and child care partnerships: Working together to serve infants, toddlers, and their families. *Young Children* 56 (3): 7–12.

Clay, J.W. 1990. Working with lesbian and gay parents and their children. *Young Children* 45 (3): 31–35.

DeJong, L. 2003. Using Erikson to work more effectively with teenage parents. *Young Children* 58 (2): 87–95.

Desrochers, J. 2001. Exploring our world: Outdoor classes for parents and children. *Young Children* 56 (5): 9–11.

Diffily, D., & K. Morrison. 1996. *Family-friendly communication for early childhood.* Washington, DC: NAEYC.

Eggers-Piérola, C. 2006. *Connections and commitments: Reflecting Latino values in early childhood programs.* Portsmouth, NH: Heinemann. Available from NAEYC.

Eldridge, D. 2001. Parent involvement: It's worth the effort. *Young Children* 56 (4): 65–69.

Elliott, E. 2003. Challenging our assumptions: Helping a baby adjust to center care. *Young Children* 58 (4): 22–28.

File, N. 2001. Family-professional partnerships: Practice that matches philosophy. *Young Children* 56 (4): 70–80.

Gadsden, V., & A. Ray. 2002. Engaging fathers: Issues and considerations for early childhood educators. *Young Children* 57 (6): 32–42.

Gadzikowski, A. 2003. It's the little things that count: How we welcome families to our full-day preschool program. *Young Children* 58 (4): 94–95.

Gennarelli, C. 2004. Family Ties. Communicating with families: Children lead the way. *Young Children* 59 (1): 98.

Gray, H. 2004. "You go away and you come back": Supporting separations and reunions in an infant/toddler classroom. *Young Children* 59 (5): 100–07.

Hannigan, I. 1998. *Off to school: A parent's-eye view of the kindergarten year.* Washington, DC: NAEYC.

Honig, A.S. 1998. *Secure relationships: Nurturing infant/toddler attachment in early care settings.* Washington, DC: NAEYC.

Joshi, A. 2005. Understanding Asian Indian families: Facilitating meaningful home-school relations. *Young Children* 60 (3): 75–78.

Kaufman, H. 2001. Skills for working with all families. *Young Children* 56 (4): 81–83.

Keyser, J. 2006. *From parents to partners: Building a family-friendly early childhood program.* St. Paul, MN: Redleaf; Washington, DC: NAEYC.

Koch, P., & M. McDonough. 1999. Improving parent-teacher conferences through collaborative conversations. *Young Children* 54 (2): 11–15.

Lundgren, D., & J.W. Morrison. 2002. Involving Spanish-speaking families in early education programs. *Young Children* 58 (3): 88–95.

McCracken, J.B. 2004. *So many goodbyes: Ways to ease the transition between home and groups for young children.* Brochure. Washington, DC: NAEYC.

Mulcahey, C. 2002. Take-home art appreciation kits for kindergartners and their families. *Young Children* 57 (1): 80–87.

Murphy, J.C. 2003. Kayla, Valencia, Franklin, and Trey: Case studies in African American school success and parenting behaviors. *Young Children* 58 (6): 85–89.

Olson, M., & M. Hyson. 2005. Supporting Teachers, Strengthening Families initiative adds a national leadership program for early childhood professionals. *Young Children* 60 (1): 44–45.

Powell, D.R. 1998. Reweaving parents into the fabric of early childhood education. *Young Children* 53 (5): 60–67.

Ray, J.A., & D. Shelton. 2004. E-pals: Connecting with families through technology. *Young Children* 59 (3): 30–32.

Reynolds, A.J., W.T. Miedel, & E.A. Mann. 2000. Innovation in early intervention for children in families with low incomes: Lessons from the Chicago Child-Parent Centers. *Young Children* 55 (2): 84–88.

Riojas-Cortez, M., B.B. Flores, & E.R. Clark. 2003. *Los niños aprenden en casa:* Valuing and connecting home cultural knowledge with an early childhood program. *Young Children* 58 (6): 78–83.

Rogers, F. 2002. *The Mister Rogers parenting book: Helping to understand your young child.* Philadelphia: Running Press. Available from NAEYC.

Rogers, F. 2003. *The world according to Mister Rogers: Important things to remember.* New York: Hyperion. Available from NAEYC.

Rosenkoetter, S.E. 2001. Come for a bedtime story! *Young Children* 56 (3): 64–66.

Rump, M.L. 2002. Involving fathers of young children with special needs. *Young Children* 57 (6): 18–20.

Simmons, C.N. 2002. Family Ties. Children's first teachers. *Young Children* 57 (3): 94–96.

Ulmen, M.C. 2005. Family Ties. Hey! Somebody read to me! Ten easy ways to include reading every day. *Young Children* 60 (6): 96.

Walker-Dalhouse, D., & A.D. Dalhouse. 2001. Parent-school relations: Communicating more effectively with African American parents. *Young Children* 56 (4): 75–80.

Wardle, F. 2001. Viewpoint. Supporting multiracial and multiethnic children and their families. *Young Children* 56 (6): 38–39.

Wickens, E. 1993. Penny's question: I will have a child in my class with two moms—What do you know about this? *Young Children* 48 (3): 25–28.

NAEYC multimedia

Grandparenting: Enriching lives. 2001. Videocassette. Prod. by Civitas. 30 min. In English or Spanish.

Partnerships with parents. 1989. Videocassette. Prod. by South Carolina Educational Television. 28 min. In English or Spanish.

Ready for life. 2000. Videocassette. Prod. by KERA in Dallas, Texas. 60 min. Features the expert advice of Dr. Bruce Perry.

The world according to Mister Rogers. 2004. CD Audio Book. Family Communications. 75 min.

Other articles and books

Berger, E.H. 2003. *Parents as partners in education: Families and schools working together.* 6th ed. Saddle River, NJ: Prentice Hall.

Chvojicek, R., M. Henthorne, & N. Larson. 2001. *Transition Magician for families: Helping parents and children with everyday routines.* St. Paul, MN: Redleaf.

Compton-Lily, C. 2002. *Reading families: The literate lives of urban children.* New York: Teachers College Press.

Davis, C., & A. Yang. 2005. *Parents and teachers working together.* Turners Falls, MA: Northeast Foundation for Children.

Dudley-Marling, C. 2000. *A family affair: When school troubles come home.* Portsmouth, NH: Heinemann.

Edwards, P.A., 1999. *A path to follow: Learning to listen to parents.* Portsmouth, NH: Heinemann.

Engaging parents and the community in schools. 1998. *Educational Leadership* 55 (8).

Epstein, J.L., M.G. Sanders, B.S. Simon, K. Clark Salinas, N.R. Jansorn, & F.L. Van Voorhis. 2002. *School, family, and community partnerships: Your handbook for action.* 2nd ed. Thousand Oaks, CA: Corwin.

Gaitan, C.D. 2004. *Involving Latino families in schools: Raising student achievement through home-school partnerships.* Thousand Oaks, CA: Corwin.

Harris Helm, J., S. Berg, P. Scranton, & R. Wilson. 2005. *Teaching parents to do projects at home.* New York: Teachers College Press.

Harry, B. 1992. *Cultural diversity, families, and the special education system.* New York: Teachers College Press.

Harry, B. 1997. *A teacher's handbook for "Cultural Diversity, Families, and the Special Education System."* New York: Teachers College Press.

Home visiting with families with infants and toddlers. 1997. *Zero to Three* 17 (4).

Huber, D. 2003. *Serving biracial and multiethnic children and their families.* St. Paul, MN: Redleaf.

Lerner, C., & A. Dombro. 2005. *Bringing up baby: Three steps to making good decisions in your child's first years.* Washington, DC: ZERO TO THREE.

Manolson, A., B. Ward, & N. Dodington. 1995. *You make the difference in helping your child learn.* Washington, DC: ZERO TO THREE.

Meier, D.R. 2000. *Scribble scrabble—Learning to read and write: Success with diverse teachers, children, and families.* New York: Teachers College Press.

National PTA. 2000. *Building successful partnerships: A guide for developing parent and family involvement programs.* Amherst, MA: National Evaluation Service.

O'Hanlon, E., & A.T. Griffin. 2004. Parent advocacy: Two approaches to change, one goal. *Leadership Development in the Infant—Family Field* 25 (2): 27–31.

Pawl, J., & A. Dombro. 2001. *Learning and growing together with families: Partnering with parents to support young children's development.* Washington, DC: ZERO TO THREE.

Power, B. 1999. *Parent power: Energizing home-school communication.* Portsmouth, NH: Heinemann.

Powers, J. 2005. *Parent-friendly early learning tips and strategies for working well with families.* St. Paul, MN: Redleaf.

Reflective practice in relationship-based organizations. 1999. *Zero to Three* 20 (1).

Responding to infants and parents. 2000. *Zero to Three* 20 (4).

Rockwell, B., & J. Rockwell Kniepkamp. 2003. *Partnering with parents: Easy programs to involve parents in the early learning process.* St. Paul, MN: Redleaf.

Taylor, D. 1998. *Family literacy: Young children learning to read and write.* Portsmouth, NH: Heinemann.

Valdes, G. 1996. *Con respeto: Bridging the distances between culturally diverse families and schools: An ethnographic portrait.* New York: Teachers College Press.

Zentella, A.C., ed. 2005. *Building on strength: Language and literacy in Latino families and communities.* New York: Teachers College Press; Covina: California Association for Bilingual Education.

Family literacy organizations

HIPPY USA (Home Instruction for Parents of Preschool Youngsters) is a parent involvement, school readiness program that helps parents prepare their three-, four-, and five-year-old children for success in school and beyond. www. hippyusa.org

National Center for Family Literacy (NCFL) helps parents and children achieve their potential together through quality literacy programs. NCFL works with educators and community builders to meet the most urgent educational needs of disadvantaged families. www.famlit.org

Reach Out and Read (ROR) is a program that promotes early literacy by bringing new books and advice about the importance of reading aloud into the pediatric exam room. Doctors and nurses give new books to children from six months of age to five years at each well-child visit. www.reachoutandread.org

Reading Is Fundamental (RIF) offers a number of programs. The National Book Program (www.rif.org/about/national book/default.mspx) motivates children,

Family Involvement Storybook Resources

Family involvement is a key component of the Harvard Family Research Project's (HFRP) (www.hfrp.org) concept of complementary learning. The concept focuses on the links between school and nonschool learning supports to foster children's learning and success.

HFRP and Reading Is Fundamental launched the online Family Involvement Storybook Corner to promote awareness and practice of family involvement through storybooks. Storybook Corner (www.gse. harvard.edu/hfrp/projects/fine/resources/storybook/index.html) provides an annotated bibliography of picture books with family involvement themes for four- to eight-year-olds.

Several of the site's resources are downloadable, and all are free. For example, tools for using the storybook *Halmoni and the Picnic* to promote involvement include a teacher lesson plan, a parent handout, and a full teacher commentary about using the storybook in the classroom, as well as a teacher training tool that uses the illustrations.

The Family Involvement Network of Educators (FINE), organized by HFRP, is another place to find family involvement resources. FINE is a community of educators, researchers, and practitioners interested in strengthening family, school, and community partnerships. Members have access to the latest, best information about family involvement; receive monthly updates about new resources; exchange ideas and insights; and learn about assessment methods for continuous improvement in family involvement practice. Membership is free. Learn more at www.gse.harvard.edu/hfrp/projects/fine.html.

families, and community members to read together. Shared Beginnings (www.rif.org/about/sharedbeginnings/default.mspx) helps young parents develop their children's early language and literacy skills. Family of Readers (www.rif.org/about/familyofreaders/default.mspx) helps parents develop the skills to support their children's reading. Running Start (www.rif. org/about/runningstart/default.mspx) is a reading motivation program for first-graders and their families. http://rif.org

Reading Rockets—For Families is a national multimedia project offering information and resources on how young children learn to read, why so many struggle, and how caring adults can help. www.readingrockets.org/families

In addition, Reading Rockets produces Colorín Colorado, www.colorincolorado.org, a Web-based source of information, activities, and advice for Spanish-speaking parents and educators of English-language learners (ELLs).

Web sites

Center on School, Family, and Community Partnerships helps families, educators, and members of communities work together to improve schools, strengthen families, and enhance student learning and development. www.csos.jhu.edu/p2000/center.htm

Early Years Are Learning Years, from NAEYC, offers short articles (suitable for newsletters) for teachers, parents, and other adults involved daily with children. www.naeyc.org/ece/eyly

Especially for Parents, from the U.S. Department of Education, provides numerous resources educators can share with parents, including a tool kit for Hispanic families. www.ed.gov/parents/anding.jhtml?src=fp

National Association of Elementary School Principals (NAESP) in 2005 published an excellent resource for administrators, *Leading Early Childhood Learning Communities: What Principals Should Know and Be Able to Do,* that describes goals for working with families. www.naesp.org/contentLoad.do?contentId=1579

National Coalition for Parent Involvement in Education advocates for the involvement of parents and families in their children's education and fosters relationships between home, school, and community. www.ncpie.org

Parent Involvement in Children's Education: Efforts by Public Elementary Schools is a report relating the findings from the Survey on Family and School Partnerships in Public Schools, K–8, conducted by National Center for Educational Statistics (NCES). The findings address a number of parent involvement topics. http://nces.ed.gov/surveys/frss/publications/98032

Parents as Teachers is an international early childhood parent education and family support program serving families of children, from pregnancy through kindergarten. www.parentsasteachers.org

ZERO TO THREE's mission is to promote the healthy development of infants and toddlers by supporting and strengthening families and communities and those who work on their behalf. The parent area of this Web site offers resources for families to engage them in their children's growth and development. www.zerotothree.org/ztt_parentAZ.html

Understanding and Involving African American Parents

Alvin F. Poussaint

IT IS IMPORTANT FOR TEACHERS to make African American children and their parents feel welcome in school. Teachers cannot be passive in this regard. African Americans often feel that public places aren't welcoming to them and might avoid school involvement because they don't feel comfortable.

African American parents sometimes think that teachers dismiss them too easily in tense situations. They may

© Karen Yoho

perceive a situation to be racist when it is not necessarily so. It is extremely important for teachers to take time to listen to families and acknowledge their concerns. For example—and this is quite common in preschool settings—a White child may ask a Black child about his or her skin color in this way: "Can't you wash the color off? Is it dirt?" If the Black child relates the comment to his parents, they may not know what to do.

We know that a comment like this from a preschooler is not racist; it is merely an expression of curiosity. However, African American adults may make negative associations when their child is told that his skin is dirty. Teachers should address such topics directly and with sensitivity: "No, the color cannot be washed off—that's the color of his skin." They can follow up by talking positively with the children about differences.

Here's another example. An African American preschooler comes home upset because some other children keep touching her hair. What may be an issue of personal space can be perceived by the parents as a racist issue, even though it is not. To prevent misunderstanding, teachers should remind the children, "We don't touch people's hair if we don't have their permission."

When these issues come up, administrators and teachers should consider forming a committee to address multiculturalism and diversity within the school. What should a teacher or a principal do if a parent says that there are not enough books or materials that represent African Americans? When families come to school, will they see pictures of diverse people—such as African American scientists or Latino artists—that might help everyone feel welcome? A committee can raise awareness of these issues and help teachers, administrators, and parents address them as they arise.

Alvin F. Poussaint, MD, is director of the Media Center of the Judge Baker Children's Center and professor of psychiatry at Harvard Medical School in Boston. He is coauthor, with James P. Comer, of *Raising Black Children.*

Susan Friedman

Reflecting, Discussing, Exploring
Questions and Follow-Up Activities

The articles in *Spotlight on Young Children and Families* represent just a small selection of the many valuable resources for early childhood educators interested in developing meaningful relationships with families. For students in early childhood professional preparation programs, for early childhood teachers taking part in training or other forms of professional development, and for other early childhood professionals, we hope these articles will provide additional ideas for understanding and engaging with families from diverse backgrounds and circumstances.

In keeping with NAEYC's Code of Ethical Conduct, which stresses that families are of primary importance in children's development, the articles promote communication, cooperation, and collaboration between home and early childhood programs in ways that enhance each child's development. These articles reflect Standard 7 of the NAEYC Early Childhood Program Standards:

> The program establishes and maintains collaborative relationships with each child's family to foster children's development in all settings. These relationships are sensitive to family composition, language, and culture.

To help you think about and expand on ideas from these articles and develop strong collaborative relationships with families, we have developed a series of questions and suggested follow-up activities. We invite you to first think about your own experiences with supporting and involving families. Questions and suggested activities related to each article then follow. Finally, we help you pull things together with general questions about family involvement, understanding and working with diverse families, resources, and next steps.

Susan Friedman, MEd, is assistant editor of *Young Children* and coordinator of **Beyond the Journal**.

A. Recalling your own early experiences

1. When you think about your own early schooling, what do you recall about your family's relationships with your teachers? In what ways did your family and teachers communicate? Did families volunteer in class, share information or stories, or attend regular meetings with teachers? What beliefs and values related to teacher-family relationships grew out of these early experiences?

2. Do you think your teachers welcomed and understood your family? Were your teachers' values different or similar to those of your family? Did your teachers accept and value your family's structure and traditions? Did classroom library books, materials, and curriculum reflect your family's culture and experiences? How do your family's experiences with your teachers relate to your views now on working with families?

B. Expanding on each article

"Understanding Families: Applying Family Systems Theory to Early Childhood Practice"/*Linda Garris Christian*

Linda Garris Christian describes family systems theory and explores six characteristics of the family as a system that are especially relevant for early childhood professionals—boundaries, roles, rules, hierarchy, climate, and equilibrium.

1. The author describes families' relationships with their children on a continuum from *disengaged* to *enmeshed*. Think of a family you have worked with or observed. Is that family closer to being enmeshed or disengaged? List some family behaviors or characteristics to support your view. How does thinking about families as primarily enmeshed or disengaged help teachers understand and better support children?

2. The author describes a situation in which a teacher noticed that a family became distant after she directed a question to the mother rather than the father, inadvertently disregarding the family's hierarchy. Think of some families with whom you have worked in the past or of your own family. How would you describe the family's hierarchy? What might you say and do to respect the hierarchy? Why is respecting a family's hierarchy important in developing and maintaining strong relationships with families?

"Partnerships for Learning: Conferencing with Families"/*Holly Seplocha*

Holly Seplocha describes parent-teacher conferences as an essential ingredient for quality early childhood education.

3. What is the goal of a parent-teacher conference? Why are conferences important? Make a chart that shows how the conference benefits the teacher, the child, and the parent.

4. Have you observed or participated in parent-teacher conferences that you think were especially successful or did not go particularly well? Describe specific parent-teacher conferences to colleagues or fellow students. If a conference did not go well, how could Seplocha's conference tips have improved it?

"Sharing the Care of Infants and Toddlers"/*Amy Laura Dombro and Claire Lerner*

Amy Laura Dombro and Claire Lerner address the uncomfortable feelings some parents may develop as their young children form close attachments to their teachers.

5. Research and develop a resource list for families about separation. Include resources about children's feelings during separation as well as those that address parents' emotions. When a teacher provides families with relevant resources, in what ways is the teacher supporting children's development?

6. Consider how relationships with families of infants and toddlers are different from those with families of older children. Reflect on new parents' needs, the emotions surrounding separation, and infant/toddler dependence on teachers. Select one unique aspect of infant/toddler care that affects the teacher-family relationship for further reading and research. Write a summary of what you learn and share it with your colleagues or classmates.

"Mapping Family Resources and Support"/*Tess Bennett*

Tess Bennett presents one tool for understanding family stresses, resources, and support networks—the family map. All families and their children come to early childhood programs with strengths and needs. The mapping process can help teachers understand family dynamics more fully.

7. Review the family map on page 21. If you were the teacher involved with the family represented, how would you use the information on the map to develop a supportive relationship with the family and to support the child's learning in the school setting? How can the mapping process help teachers support children's learning?

8. The author describes teachers as part of the resource networks of families—with either a positive or a negative effect on family functioning. For example, if a teacher takes over for a family in a crisis, initiating and completing tasks the family could do, the family may not feel capable in a future crisis. How could the teacher connect a family with resources in a more positive way? Give examples of positive and negative ways teachers can help families connect to support networks in the community.

"Creating Safe, Just Places to Learn for Children of Lesbian and Gay Parents"/*James W. Clay*

A preschool director uses a questionnaire and phone interviews to gain an understanding of lesbian and gay families' perspectives about preschool and their concerns and goals for their children.

9. What were the main concerns about their children that lesbian and gay parents expressed through the survey and phone interviews? How might a teacher whose class includes children of lesbian/gay families address some of those concerns? Develop a plan the teacher could use to ensure that all children feel fully included in the classroom community.

10. Teachers need to pay attention to every family's desire to belong to a larger community. List the ways that the program described in this article fosters a sense of community among families. What other ways could a program or school create a caring community? Compare your list with those of colleagues or classmates.

"A Team Approach: Supporting Families of Children with Disabilities in Inclusive Programs"/*Louise A. Kaczmarek*

Louise Kaczmarek presents strategies for supporting families of children with disabilities in inclusive settings, including frequent communication between home and school and identification of useful community resources.

11. Think of a program in which you have worked or observed. If the program began including children with special needs, what additions to family-school communication would be needed? If the program already includes children with special needs, what improvements could be made to family-school communications?

12. One of the author's recommendations is to provide families with resources to connect them with community organizations and services. Consider the special needs and the cultural backgrounds of the children and families in one particular class. Draft a list of community organizations that could offer support to that group of families.

"Closing the Gap: Culture and the Promotion of Inclusion in Child Care"/*Jennifer Bradley and Peris Kibera*

Jennifer Bradley and Peris Kibera analyze how an understanding of families' cultural backgrounds supports the success of programs in providing inclusive care for diverse children with disabilities or challenging behaviors.

13. On page 40 the authors provide questions that teachers can use to learn about four dimensions of culture. Select a child from your class or from a class in which you have observed and answer as many of these questions as you can about the child's family. What have you learned about the family's culture by using this tool? How might the information help a teacher support the child's learning?

14. A preschooler has become increasingly aggressive with his peers. How might the teacher invite the child's family to share their observations and insights about the change in their child's behavior while still respecting their privacy? What should the teacher consider before asking? For example, the teacher could consider the family's hierarchy and culture. Discuss your ideas with colleagues or other students.

"Reading Their Worlds: Working with Diverse Families to Enhance Children's Early Literacy Development"/ *Rosario Ordoñez-Jasis and Robert W. Ortiz*

Rosario Ordoñez-Jasis and Robert Ortiz explain why educators need to respect the diversity of children's home-based literacy knowledge.

15. The authors describe (1) the deficit perspective, in which educators do not "fully recognize, incorporate, or tap into the wealth of literacy information, skills, and knowledge that parents may hold;" and (2) the information-gathering approach, in which educators "view parents as providers of information" who can support their child's literacy development. How does the second approach benefit children and families? Give some examples of contributions all families can make to their children's literacy efforts.

16. Families support their children's literacy development in many ways—engaging children in conversations, reading to them, telling folktales. Review the box "Basics for a Family Survey" (p. 45). Draft a survey for a particular group of parents. Using the survey, interview two families. What have you learned about the families' involvement in their children's literacy learning? Discuss the similarities and differences.

Leave No Parent Behind: Three Proven Strategies
"Leaps and Bounds: Preparing Parents for Kindergarten"/*Michelle Rhodes, Billie Enz, and Marilyn LaCount*
"Home Connections to Learning: Supporting Parents as Teachers"/*Yvette Mass and Kathleen Ann Cohan*
"Virtual Pre-K: Connecting Home, School, and Community"/*Alicia Narvaez, Jessica Feldman, and Christopher Theriot*

Three approaches, while different, all encourage families to engage their children in home learning activities that build on what takes place in the program or school.

17. After reading the three articles, make a chart showing the goals and the in-school and at-home components of each program. Describe how each program supports family involvement and promotes children's development and learning. Using the chart, explain to a colleague or classmate how the programs are alike and how they differ.

18. Select one of the three programs and write a sample activity for families. For example, if a math activity is based on recognizing patterns, the at-home activity could have adults and children look around their home to identify patterns and then create their own. Describe the in-class component, the activity for families, the age of the children, and the curriculum area addressed. Share your activity with colleagues or fellow students.

"Family Involvement in an International School: Piloting a Parent-Teacher Reading Group"/*Gail Wentworth*

Gail Wentworth describes a monthly reading group formed in response to families' interest in understanding developmentally appropriate practice and their need to be part of a community.

19. Wentworth and a colleague began the reading group to answer parents' questions about the curriculum, to explain developmentally appropriate practice, and to build community. How does the reading group model address these three goals?

20. Write a letter inviting families to participate in a reading group. Based on the ages of the children and on the families' concerns and interests, create a suggested reading list for your group. Compare and discuss your list and letter with others. How did the lists and letters differ in relation to the children's ages, the families' cultures, or family structure?

C. Making connections

Consider the big picture

1. In your view, what are the three most important themes or key ideas recurring across these articles? If possible, compare your nominations with those of other readers.

2. As you think about the articles, consider the importance of understanding and valuing culture when supporting and involving families in meaningful ways. How does culture come into play in communicating with families? In getting to know families? When inviting families to share information about their child?

3. Because this is a small selection of articles, some important principles may have been omitted. What aspects of understanding and working with families do you feel are underrepresented or missing? What components of working with families does your program, school, state, or local district require that are missing here?

Examine curriculum goals and expected outcomes

4. Read these sections from two NAEYC position statements, which stress the importance of positive working relationships with families:

   • Establishing Reciprocal Relationships with Families, from "Developmentally Appropriate Practice in Early Childhood Programs Serving Children from Birth through Age 8" (**www.naeyc.org/about/ positions/dap4.asp**).

   • Where We Stand—Many Languages, Many Cultures: Respecting and Responding to Diversity (**www.naeyc. org/about/positions/pdf/diversity.pdf**), adapted from "Responding to Linguistic and Cultural Diversity: Recommendations for Effective Early Childhood Education"

   Discuss these documents with a group of colleagues or fellow students. Individuals could choose certain recommendations or examples to present to the rest of the group.

5. It is critical to weave families' cultures into many aspects of the classroom environment and curriculum. Consider your state's standards (to find them, try the National Institute for Early Education Research Web site at http://nieer.org/standards/statelist.php or the SERVE report Web site at www.serve.org/ELO/research. html). In what ways can teachers create a multicultural learning environment and ensure that the curriculum reflects all families' characteristics and cultures?

6. What guidelines does your school district, school, or program provide for working with families? What are the policies and practices for parent-teacher conferences? What services, supports, and information, if any, does your school or program make available to families?

7. Working with colleagues or fellow students, compare some of the applicable guidelines for working with families. How are they similar and different? How useful are such materials in guiding your practice? Which methods described in these articles (for example, family map, family survey) would you recommend be included in these guidelines?

Use reflection to enhance teaching practices

8. As you read and discuss the articles, what do you find that affirms your practice? What questions do the articles raise about your current approaches to working with families? What new approaches might you try?

9. What kinds of supports do teachers need to engage in reciprocal relationships with families, working toward cooperation, shared responsibility, and negotiation of conflicts to achieve shared goals? Describe the characteristics of a program or school in which teachers and families can develop and maintain meaningful relationships that support children's learning.

10. Review Standard 7 of the NAEYC Early Childhood Program Standards (**www.naeyc.org/academy/standards/standard7**). Consider the accreditation criteria for the following topic areas as they relate to your work with families and their children: (1) Knowing and Understanding the Program's Families; (2) Sharing Information Between Staff and Families; and (3) Nurturing Families as Advocates for their Children. Reflect on how well you meet these criteria in your current practice. Note any areas that need improvement and develop a plan to address these areas.

Focus on families and communities

11. One way to learn about families is to ask them questions by means of a questionnaire or survey. For the families you have worked with or observed, what information could help you support their children's development and learning? Draft a family survey that addresses this information. Share your survey with colleagues or fellow students.

12. Review the curriculum and daily plans for your class or a class you have observed. How could you include families in the many aspects of the program—literacy, music, creative arts, social studies, mathematics, and science? Select one content area and develop a plan for involving families. Implement your plan.

Identify resources and plan next steps

13. The resources section (pp. 58–60) contains rich lists of books, articles, and Web sites related to supporting and involving families. Select several resources and write annotated descriptions to guide others, perhaps formatting the information as a handout or a Web page. For which professionals is the list particularly valuable? For which families?

14. What do you want to know more about in order to better support and involve families? What will you want to change in your practice?

15. Develop specific plans to enhance parent-teacher conferences. Create an action plan to guide this work. What would you need to do? Consider any questionnaires or materials you will need to create to pass on to families before the conference. Implement your plans.

naeyc Promoting excellence in early childhood education

Since 1926

National Association for the Education of Young Children

1313 L Street NW, Suite 500, Washington, DC 20005-4101   202-232-8777   800-424-2460   Fax 202-328-1846

www.naeyc.org

February 1, 2007

Dear Comprehensive Member:

Struck by the strong interest in our Spotlight books, I decided to choose as the first benefit of the new year this volume, *Spotlight on Young Children and Families*. It is edited by Derry Koralek, the editor of *Young Children* and originator of this popular series of resources.

Like the other volumes in our Spotlight series, this collection of articles provides faculty members, trainers, and students with many timely topics of discussion relating to a theme. This time the focus is on issues and practices relating to families, such as promoting inclusion, acknowledging and valuing all cultures and kinds of families, and establishing connections between home and school. And, as always, there also are interactive questions and activities for reflection and discussion, as well as a valuable list of key resources. If you are not already familiar with the Spotlight books, I hope you will visit our Web site at www.naeyc.org to see others in the series.

Sincerely,

Carol Copple

Carol Copple
Publications Editor, Books